The Easy Interpre

通訳する本
The Easy Interpreter

A Japanese phrasebook for the hospitality industry

Second Edition

**Yoko Pinkerton and
Masumi Hiraga**

Hospitality Press, Melbourne

Hospitality Press Pty Ltd
38 Riddell Parade
P.O. Box 426
Elsternwick Vic 3185 Australia
Phone (03) 9528 5021 Fax (03) 9528 2645

Second edition 1998

Pinkerton, Yoko.
   The easy interpreter: a Japanese phrasebook for
the hospitality industry.

   2nd ed.
   Includes index.
   ISBN 1 86250 460 1.

   1. Japanese language — Conversation and phrase
books — English. 2. Japanese language — Conversation
and phrase books (for restaurant and hotel personnel).
   I. Hiraga, Masumi. II. Title.

495.683421

Designed by John van Loon

Printed in Australia by Impact Printing Pty Ltd, Brunswick, Vic.
Published by Hospitality Press Pty Ltd, Melbourne

Contents

Introduction

All too often people working in the tourism and hospitality industry experience the frustration of being unable to communicate effectively with their Japanese guests for want of the appropriate phrases in Japanese. The problem is that most existing word and phrase books are designed to aid only the tourist, listing questions such as 'How long will it take?' The orientation of *The Easy Interpreter* is different because it contains expressions that people dealing with tourists may wish to use, for example 'It'll take half an hour'. It is therefore the first English-Japanese phrase book designed to assist non-Japanese-speaking staff.

The authors have combined their knowledge as language specialists with extensive experience in the tourism and hospitality industry to produce a careful selection of words and phrases applicable to each situation described in this book. We hope that *The Easy Interpreter* will facilitate essential communication between you and your Japanese guests.

Yoko Pinkerton
Masumi Hiraga

How to use this book

Find the phrase you need instantly!

The 21 chapters contain 1000 phrases grouped under subheadings. Use these subheadings as an index to help you find the phrase you need. A full indexed vocabulary list is supplied at the back of the book.

How to use the word list

Chapters 2-21 each begin with a list of the fifty most useful relevant words in Japanese. You can treat the list as a glossary or as a means of communicating with Japanese tourists, using the absolute minimum vocabulary.

How do I pronounce the words?

Japanese is relatively easy to pronounce. Consult the guide to pronunciation and attempt to pronounce the words or phrases listed in the romanized version.

Alternatively you could use the accompanying Japanese script to point out the desired word or phrase to a Japanese tourist.

What if I can't find the word I need?

Many English words have been incorporated into the Japanese language, words such as knife, fork, cup, napkin, milk. We cannot list them all here, but they are of a sufficient number to warrant your trying out English words in cases of real difficulty. If you take care to place equal stress on each syllable of the word and do not drop any sounds, e.g. FO-R-K, not for(k); NA-PU-KI-N, not na(p)ki(n), then in many instances Japanese people will understand you. (And in this way you can increase your Japanese vocabulary!)

Is what I am saying polite enough?

Yes! We use in this book the standard formal speech, which is sufficiently polite for any spoken situation. In specific situations however, such as attending guests/customers at hotels or in shops, or when you are apologizing or making a request, it may be more appropriate to use an extra polite form. In this case, simply begin the sentence with SUMIMASENGA (meaning Excuse me/Pardon me/I'm sorry/Sorry to bother you, etc.). For example, by extending the phrase KOCHIRA NI KITE KUDASAI (Please come this way) to SUMIMASENGA, KOCHIRA NI KITE KUDASAI, you are saying, 'Would you mind coming this way, please?'

A word of warning

The phrases in this book are intended for conversational use only. If you wish to use particular phrases for public display (for example at a shop or hotel counter), first consult a Japanese language expert. As the purpose changes, so does the wording.

Pronunciation of Japanese

The pronunciation of Japanese is relatively easy. Here are some important points to remember.

1
	Vowels	Pronounced as in:	Hold these sounds twice as long
	a	b*a*llet	aa
	e	y*e*s	ee
	i	w*i*nk	ii
	o	s*o*ld	oo
	u	b*u*sh	uu

2 Each syllable is pronounced separately and given equal stress. Be careful not to drop any sounds.
e.g. O/SO/I (late, slow)
MI/RU/KU (milk)

3 Do not stress sharply as you do in English. Japanese has a more even sound than English.
e.g. O/KA/E/RI/NA/SA/I (Welcome back!)
BA/TO/MIN/TON (badminton)

4 The pronunciation of 'r' is close to the English 'l'.
e.g. RIRAKKUSU (relax) = LILAKKUSU
RESUTORAN (restaurant) = LESUTOLAN

Calling a telephone interpreter

ENGLISH	ROMANIZED JAPANESE	JAPANESE
I'll get a telephone interpreter.	Denwa tsuuyaku o tanomimashoo.	電話通訳を頼みましょう。
An interpreter will be available in one hour.	Tsuuyaku ga mitsukaru made ichijikan gurai kakarimasu.	通訳が見つかるまで1時間位かかります。
The interpreter is on the phone.	Tsuuyaku ga denwa ni dete imasu.	通訳が電話に出ています。
Please speak in Japanese.	Nihongo de hanashite kudasai.	日本語で話して下さい。
Let me speak when you are finished.	Hanashi owattara watashi ga kawarimasu.	話し終わったら私がかわります。
An interpreter is not available at the moment.	Tsuuyaku wa ima mitsukarimasen.	通訳は今見つかりません。
I'll try again later.	Mata atode kakemashoo.	又、あとでかけましょう。

1 Useful expressions

	ENGLISH	ROMANIZED JAPANESE	JAPANESE
1	Hello.	Konnichiwa.	こんにちは。
2	Good morning.	Ohayoo gozaimasu.	おはようございます。
3	Good evening.	Konbanwa.	こんばんは。
4	Mr/Mrs/Ms/Miss Tanaka	Tanaka-san	田中さん
5	Are you Mr/Mrs/Ms/Miss Tanaka?	Tanaka-san desu ka?	田中さんですか。
6	Is Mr/Mrs/Ms/Miss Tanaka here?	Tanaka-san wa irasshaimasu ka?	田中さんはいらっしゃいますか。
7	Good-bye.	Sayoonara.	さようなら。
8	Good-night.	Oyasuminasai.	おやすみなさい。
9	See you again.	Dewa mata.	では又。
10	See you tomorrow.	Mata ashita.	又あした。
11	Take care.	Oki o tsukete.	お気をつけて。
12	Have a good trip.	Yoi goryokoo o.	よいご旅行を。

	ENGLISH	ROMANIZED JAPANESE	JAPANESE
13	Have a nice time.	Tanoshinde kudasai.	楽しんで下さい。
14	Please give my regards to Mr Tanaka.	Tanaka-san ni yoroshiku.	田中さんによろしく。
15	Yes.	Hai.	はい。
16	No.	Iie.	いいえ。
17	Yes, it is. /That's all right.	Hai, soo desu.	はい、そうです。
18	No, it isn't. /That's not right.	Iie, chigaimasu.	いいえ、ちがいます。
19	It's all right. /You may do so.	Ii desu.	いいです。
20	There is. /We have.	Arimasu.	あります。
21	There isn't. /We don't have.	Arimasen.	ありません。
22	Thank you.	Arigatoo.	ありがとう。
23	Thank you very much.	Arigatoo gozaimasu.	ありがとうございます。
24	It's a pleasure.	Doo itashimashite.	どういたしまして。

	ENGLISH	ROMANIZED JAPANESE	JAPANESE
25	Congratulations.	Omedetoo gozaimasu.	おめでとうございます。
26	I'm glad to be of help.	Oyaku ni tatete ureshii desu.	お役に立ててうれしいです。
27	Please come again.	Mata doozo.	又どうぞ。
28	I'm sorry.	Sumimasen.	すみません。
29	Excuse me./Pardon me.	Shitsurei shimasu.	しつれいします。
30	Sorry (for what happened).	Shitsurei shimashita.	しつれいしました。
31	We/I made a mistake.	Machigaemashita.	間違えました。
32	Sorry to have kept you waiting.	Omatase shimashita.	お待たせしました。
33	It's here.	Koko desu.	ここです。
34	It's not here.	Koko dewa arimasen.	ここではありません。
35	It's over there.	Asoko desu.	あそこです。
36	This way.	Kochira desu.	こちらです。
37	After you.	Doozo osaki ni.	どうぞお先に。

	ENGLISH	ROMANIZED JAPANESE	JAPANESE
38	Please come in./Enter.	Doozo ohairi kudasai.	どうぞお入り下さい。
39	Welcome (to shop/house).	Irasshaimase.	いらっしゃいませ。
40	How are you? /How would you like it?	Ikaga desu ka?	いかがですか。
41	Is this all right?/Do you like this?	Yoroshii desu ka?	よろしいですか。
42	Is anything the matter?	Dooka shimashita ka?	どうかしましたか。
43	I'll show you the way.	Goannai shimashoo.	ご案内しましょう。
44	I'll take you there.	Otsure shimashoo.	お連れしましょう。
45	It's $10.	Juudoru desu.	10ドルです。
46	It's expensive.	Takai desu.	高いです。
47	It's not expensive.	Takakunai desu.	高くないです。
48	It's cheap.	Yasui desu.	安いです。
49	It costs more.	Shooshoo takai desu.	少々高いです。

	ENGLISH	ROMANIZED JAPANESE	JAPANESE
50	There is a charge.	**Yuuryoo desu.**	有料です。
51	It's free of charge.	Muryoo desu.	無料です。
52	Please.	Doozo.	どうぞ。
53	Please do (so).	Onegai shimasu.	お願いします。
54	Wait a moment, please.	Shooshoo omachi kudasai.	少々お待ち下さい。
55	Please speak slowly.	Yukkuri hanashite kudasai.	ゆっくり話して下さい。
56	Will you come with me, please.	Watashi to isshoni kite kudasai.	私と一緒に来て下さい。
57	Please write in English.	Eigo de kaite kudasai.	英語で書いて下さい。
58	I/We understand.	Wakarimashita.	分かりました。
59	I/We don't understand.	Wakarimasen.	分かりません。
60	Do you understand?	Wakarimasu ka?	分かりますか。
61	Do you understand English?	Eigo ga wakarimasu ka?	英語が分かりますか。

14

	ENGLISH	ROMANIZED JAPANESE	JAPANESE
62	I don't understand Japanese.	Nihongo ga wakarimasen.	日本語が分かりません。
63	Please be careful./Look out, please.	Ki o tsukete kudasai.	気をつけて下さい。
64	It's dangerous.	Abunai desu.	あぶないです。
65	I'll be back soon./I won't be long.	Sugu kimasu.	すぐ来ます。
66	It's non-smoking.	Kin'en desu.	禁煙です。
67	Please hurry.	Isoide kudasai.	いそいで下さい。
68	Don't worry.	Goshinpai naku.	ご心配なく。
69	That's not possible.	Sore wa muri desu.	それは無理です。
70	Is that/are you all right?	Daijoobu desu ka?	大丈夫ですか。
71	Who are you?	Donata desu ka?	どなたですか。
72	Where is it?	Doko desu ka?	どこですか。
73	What is it?	Nan desu ka?	何ですか。

Useful expressions

	ENGLISH	ROMANIZED JAPANESE	JAPANESE
74	When is it?	Itsu desu ka?	いつですか。
75	Why?	Dooshite desu ka?	どうしてですか。
76	At what time?	Nanji ni?	何時に。
77	How much is it? (price)	Ikura desu ka?	いくらですか。
78	Which one?	Dochira desu ka?	どちらですか。
79	How many?	Ikutsu desu ka?	いくつですか。
80	How much/long? (quantity, distance, etc.)	Dono kurai desu ka?	どの位ですか。

2 On the plane

[1] See also 4. Departure and luggage: Seat allocation.
[2] See also 13. At the restaurant: Beverages, Finding out
customer preferences.
[3] See also 14. Shopping: Duty-free goods.

ENGLISH	ROMANIZED JAPANESE	JAPANESE
On the plane	Kinai	機内
Boarding pass	Toojooken	塔乗券
Seat	Seki/Zaseki	席、座席
Vacant seat	Kuuseki	空席
Full seat	Manseki	満席
Wrong seat	Machigatta seki	間違った席
Cigarette	Tabako	タバコ
Non-smoking	Kin'en	禁煙
Non-smoking section	Kin'enseki	禁煙席
Smoking	Kitsuen	喫煙
Seat belt	Shiitoberuto	シートベルト
Flight	Bin/Furaito	便、フライト
Luggage	Nimotsu	荷物
Cabin luggage	Kinai mochikomi nimotsu	機内持ち込み荷物
Floor	Yuka	床
Seat at the front	Mae no seki	前の席

ENGLISH	ROMANIZED JAPANESE	JAPANESE
Seat at the back	Ushiro no seki	後ろの席
Locker	Rokkaa	ロッカー
Call button	Kooru botan	コールボタン
Blanket	Moofu	毛布
Pillow	Makura	枕
Toilet	Toire/Otearai	トイレ、お手洗い
Occupied	Shiyoochuu	使用中
Bassinet	Yoojiyoo beddo	幼児用ベッド
Drink	Nomimono	飲み物
Free of charge	Muryoo	無料
Japanese newspaper	Nihongo no shinbun	日本語の新聞
Film (movie)	Eiga	映画
Duty-free goods	Menzeihin	免税品
Non-taxable	Muzei	無税
Alcohol	Sakerui	酒類
Japanese yen	Nihon'en	日本円

ENGLISH	ROMANIZED JAPANESE	JAPANESE
Medicine	Kusuri	薬
Air-sickness bag	**Echiketto-bukuro**	**エチケット袋**
Meal	Shokuji	食事
Customs declaration card	Zeikan shinkokusho	税関申告書
Immigration card	Nyuukoku kaado	入国カード
Transit	Noritsugi	乗り継ぎ
Transit pass	Tsuuka pasu	通過パス
Airline ticket	Kookuuken	航空券
Aircraft	Hikooki	飛行機
Air hostess/Flight attendant	Suchuwadesu /Joomuin	スチュワーデス、乗務員
Local time	Genchi jikan	現地時間
Time difference	Jisa	時差
Arrival	Toochaku	到着
Landing	Chakuriku	着陸
Emergency exit	Hijooguchi	非常口
Oxygen mask	Sanso masuku	酸素マスク

ENGLISH	ROMANIZED JAPANESE	JAPANESE
Life jacket	Kyuumei dooi	救命胴衣
Due to fog	Kiri no tame	霧のため

	ENGLISH	ROMANIZED JAPANESE	JAPANESE
81	Please show me your boarding pass.	Toojooken o haiken shimasu.	搭乗券を拝見します。
82	This is your seat.	Ozaseki wa kochira desu.	お座席はこちらです。
83	You may sit here.	Kono seki ni osuwari kudasai.	この席にお座り下さい。
84	You are occupying the wrong seat.	Ozaseki ga machigatte imasu.	お座席が間違っています。
85	Please change to the seat over there.	Achira no seki to kawatte kudasaimasen ka.	あちらの席とかわって下さいませんか。
86	This is a non-smoking seat.	Koko wa kin'enseki desu.	ここは禁煙席です。
87	You may move to a smoking seat.	Kitsuenseki ni utsuraremasu ka.	喫煙席に移られますか。
88	Please put your seat up.	Shiito o tatete kudasai.	シートを立てて下さい。
89	Please fasten your seat belt.	Shiitoberuto o shite kudasai.	シートベルトをして下さい。
90	This is too big.	Kore wa ooki sugimasu.	これは大きすぎます。

	ENGLISH	ROMANIZED JAPANESE	JAPANESE
91	You can't take this as cabin luggage.	Kinai mochikomi wa dekimasen.	機内持ち込みはできません。
92	We will look after this for you.	Kochira de oazukari shimasu.	こちらでお預かりします。
93	You may not put that luggage on the floor.	Nimotsu wa yuka ni okanai yoo ni onegai shimasu.	荷物は床に置かないように お願いします。
94	Please put that luggage under the seat in front.	Nimotsu wa mae no seki no shita ni oire kudasai.	荷物は前の席の下においれ 下さい。
95	Let me put this in the locker.	Rokkaa ni iremashoo.	ロッカーに入れましょう。
96	This is your call button.	Kore wa kooru botan desu.	これはコールボタンです。
97	Did you call me?	Oyobi ni narimashita ka?	お呼びになりましたか。
98	Shall I get you a blanket?	Moofu o otori shimashoo ka?	毛布をお取りしましょうか。
99	Do you need another pillow?	Makura ga moohitotsu irimasu ka?	枕がもうひとつ要りますか。
100	The toilet is occupied.	Toire wa shiyoochuu desu.	トイレは使用中です。

	ENGLISH	ROMANIZED JAPANESE	JAPANESE
101	You cannot use the toilet now.	Ima toire wa tsukaemasen.	今トイレは使えません。
102	Would you like ear-phones?	Iyahon o otsukai ni narimasu ka?	イヤホンをお使いになりますか。
103	Would you like to have a drink?	Onomimono wa ikaga desu ka?	お飲み物はいかがですか。
104	This is free of charge.	Kore wa muryoo saabisu desu.	これは無料サービスです。
105	We don't have Japanese newspapers.	Nihongo no shinbun wa arimasen.	日本語の新聞はありません。
106	A film will be shown after the meal.	Shokuji no ato eiga ga arimasu.	食事のあと映画があります。
107	The film is on channel 2.	Eiga wa nichan'neru desu.	映画は2チャンネルです。
108	We are selling duty-free goods.	Menzeihin no hanbai desu.	免税品の販売です。
109	The alcohol is duty-free up to 3 bottles.	Osake wa sanbon made muzei desu.	お酒は3本まで無税です。

	ENGLISH	ROMANIZED JAPANESE	JAPANESE
110	We take travellers cheques.	Toraberaazu chekku ga tsukaemasu.	トラベラーズチェックが使えます。
111	We accept Japanese yen.	Nihon'en de haraemasu.	日本円で払えます。
112	We don't have that brand.	Sono burando wa arimasen.	そのブランドはありません。
113	Are you not feeling well?	Gokibun demo warui desu ka?	ご気分でも悪いですか。
114	Would you like some medicine to stop air sickness?	Yoidome no kusuri o sashiagemashoo ka?	よい止めの薬をさしあげましょうか。
115	There is an air-sickness bag in here.	Echiketto-bukuro wa koko ni haitte imasu.	エチケット袋はここに入っています。
116	How are you feeling?	Gokibun wa ikaga desu ka?	ご気分はいかがですか。
117	Are you feeling any better?	Sukoshi yoku narimashita ka?	少しよくなりましたか。
118	Aren't you eating anything?	Nani mo meshiagarimasen ka?	何も召し上がりませんか。
119	Please fill in the immigration card.	Nyuukoku kaado o kinyuu shite kudasai.	入国カードを記入して下さい。

	ENGLISH	ROMANIZED JAPANESE	JAPANESE
120	Please fill in the customs declaration form.	Zeikan shinkokusho o kinyuu shite kudasai.	税関申告書を記入して下さい。
121	The local time is 4 o'clock.	Genchi jikan wa yoji desu.	現地時間は4時です。
122	Are you a transit passenger?	Noritsugi desu ka?	乗り継ぎですか。
123	Please show me your airline ticket.	**Kookuuken o haiken shimasu.**	航空券を拝見します。
124	You must get off the plane.	Kinai kara denakutewa narimasen.	機内から出なくてはなりません。
125	Please take your luggage with you.	Nimotsu o motte orite kudasai.	荷物を持って降りて下さい。
126	The seat allocation will be changed.	Zaseki ga kawarimasu.	座席がかわります。
127	Is there a tour escort?	Tenjooin wa imasu ka?	添乗員はいますか。
128	The aircraft cannot land at Sydney.	Hikooki wa Shidonii ni chakuriku dekimasen.	飛行機はシドニーに着陸できません。
129	London Airport is closed due to fog.	Kiri no tame Rondon kuukoo wa heisachuu desu.	霧のため、ロンドン空港は閉鎖中です。

3 Arrival and Customs

[1] See also 21. Accidents and emergency: Lost property, We'll contact you.

ENGLISH	ROMANIZED JAPANESE	JAPANESE
Arrival	Toochaku	到着
Customs	Zeikan	税関
Immigration routine	Nyuukoku shinsa	入国審査
Passport	Ryoken/Pasupooto	旅券、パスポート
Visa	Sashoo/Biza	査証、ビザ
Airline ticket	Kookuuken	航空券
Return ticket (both ways)	Oofukuken	往復券
Disembarkation card	Nyuukoku kaado	入国カード
Non-resident	Hikyojuusha	非居住者
Place of departure	Shuppatsuchi	出発地
Destination	Mokutekichi	目的地
Purpose of visit	Tokoo mokuteki	渡航目的
Holiday	Kankoo	観光
Business trip	Shooyoo	商用
A letter of acceptance (from an educational institution)	Nyuugaku kyokasho	入学許可書

ENGLISH	ROMANIZED JAPANESE	JAPANESE
Place you intend to stay	Taizaisaki	滞在先
Duration of stay	Taizainissuu	滞在日数
Form	Yooshi	用紙
Nationality	Kokuseki	国籍
Date of birth	Seinengappi	生年月日
Full name	Shimei	氏名
Family name	Myooji	名字
Age	Nenrei	年令
Address	Genjuusho	現住所
Occupation	Shokugyoo	職業
Married	Kikon	既婚
Not married	Mikon/Dokushin	未婚、独身
Signature	Shomei	署名
Luggage	Nimotsu	荷物
Luggage claim tag	Nimotsu hikikaeshoo	荷物引替証
Name tag	Nafuda	名札

ENGLISH	ROMANIZED JAPANESE	JAPANESE
Things left behind	Wasuremono	忘れ物
Lost property	Ishitsubutsu gakari	遺失物係
Lost	Funshitsu	紛失
Damaged	Hason	破損
Compensation	Benshoo	弁償
Procedure	Tetsuzuki	手続き
Customs officer	Nyuukoku shinsakan	入国審査官
Customs declaration	Zeikan shinkoku	税関申告
Inspection	Kensa	検査
Customs duty	Kanzei	関税
Personal effects	Mi no mawarihin	身のまわり品
Processed food	Kakooshokuhin	加工食品
Quarantine	Ken'eki	検疫
Vaccination certificate	Yoboosesshu shoomeisho	予防接種証明書
Yellow fever	Oonetsubyoo	黄熱病
Cholera	Korera	コレラ

ENGLISH	ROMANIZED JAPANESE	JAPANESE
Typhoid fever	Chifusu	チフス
Prohibited article	Mochikomi kinshihin	持ち込み禁止品
Confiscation	Bosshuu	没収

	ENGLISH	ROMANIZED JAPANESE	JAPANESE
130	Please wait in this queue.	Kono retsu ni narande kudasai.	この列に並んで下さい。
131	Please wait in the queue for non-residents.	Hikyojuushayoo no retsu ni narande kudasai.	非居住者用の列に並んで下さい。
132	May I see your passport?	Pasupooto o misete kudasai.	パスポートを見せて下さい。
133	Please show me your airline ticket.	Kookuuken o misete kudasai.	航空券を見せて下さい。
134	Can I have your immigration card?	Nyuukoku kaado o misete kudasai.	入国カードを みせて 下さい。
135	Are you on a group tour?	Dantai ryokoo desu ka?	団体旅行ですか。
136	Where is your tour escort?	Tenjooin wa doko desu ka?	添乗員はどこですか。
137	Are you on your own?	Ohitori desu ka?	おひとりですか。
138	How long do you intend to stay?	Taizai kikan wa dono kurai desu ka?	滞在期間はどの位ですか。
139	Are you here for a holiday?	Kankoo ryokoo desu ka?	観光旅行ですか。

	ENGLISH	ROMANIZED JAPANESE	JAPANESE
140	Are you on business?	Shooyoo desu ka?	商用ですか。
141	Please show me the letter of acceptance (from an educational institution).	Nyuugaku kyokasho o misete kudasai.	入学許可書を見せて下さい。
142	Where do you intend to stay?	Shukuhaku basho wa doko desu ka?	宿泊場所はどこですか。
143	I must have a further check.	Moosukoshi shirabe sasete kudasai.	もう少し調べさせて下さい。
144	Please come with me to the officer-in-charge.	Watashi to issho ni kakari no hitono tokoro ni kite kudasai.	私と一緒に係の人のところに来て下さい。
145	That is all right.	Hai. Kekkoo desu.	はい、結構です。
146	Please go through.	Doozo otoori kudasai.	どうどお通り下さい。
147	Please collect your luggage over there.	Nimotsu no uketori basho wa achira desu.	荷物の受け取り場所はあちらです。
148	Please go to the carousel showing the number of the flight you were on.	Jibun no notte kita binmei no tokoro ni itte kudasai.	自分の乗って来た便名のところに行って下さい。

	ENGLISH	ROMANIZED JAPANESE	JAPANESE
149	Please go to the lost property counter.	Ishitsubutsu gakari ni itte kudasai.	遺失物係に行って下さい。
150	May I see your luggage claim tag?	Nimotsu no hikikaeshoo o misete kudasai.	荷物の引替証を見せて下さい。
151	Please wait here for a moment.	Shibaraku koko de matte kudasai.	しばらくここで待って下さい。
152	We are checking now.	Ima shirabete imasu.	今、調べています。
153	I'll get a person who speaks Japanese.	Nihongo ga hanaseru hito o tsurete kimasu.	日本語が話せる人を連れて来ます。
154	How big is the suitcase?	Suutsukeesu no ookisa wa dono kurai desu ka?	スーツケースの大きさはどの位ですか。
155	What colour is it?	Nani iro desu ka?	何色ですか。
156	Does it have your name tag?	Nafuda wa tsuite imasu ka?	名札はついていますか。
157	Does the suitcase have wheels?	Suutsukeesu ni kuruma ga tsuite imasu ka?	スーツケースに車がついていますか。

	ENGLISH	ROMANIZED JAPANESE	JAPANESE
158	What is in the suitcase?	Suutsukeesu no nakami wa nan desu ka?	スーツケースの中味は何で すか。
159	We'll contact you as soon as we find it.	**Mitsukari shidai gorenraku shimasu.**	見つかり次第ご連絡します。
160	Please fill in this form.	Kono yooshi ni kinyuu shite kudasai.	この用紙に記入して下さい。
161	Please come to the airport to collect it when you are notified.	Renraku ga attara kuukoo ni tori ni kite kudasai.	連絡があったら空港に取り に来て下さい。
162	You must bring the key to open the suitcase for inspection.	Nimotsu no kensa no tame ni kagi o motte kite kudasai.	荷物の検査のために鍵を持 って来て下さい。
163	Please have your luggage checked over there.	Asoko de nimotsu no kensa o ukete kudasai.	あそこで荷物の検査を受け て下さい。
164	Please open the suitcase.	Suutsukeesu o akete kudasai.	スーツケースを開けて下さ い。

	ENGLISH	ROMANIZED JAPANESE	JAPANESE
165	Please give me your customs declaration.	Zeikan shinkokusho o dashite kudasai.	税関申告書を出して下さい。
166	Do you have anything to declare?	Shinkoku suru mono wa arimasen ka?	申告するものはありませんか。
167	You must declare all of these.	Kore wa zenbu shinkoku shinakereba narimasen.	これは全部申告しなければなりません。
168	These are not taxable even if you declare them.	Shinkoku shitemo kazei saremasen.	申告しても課税されません。
169	Do you have any alcohol or cigarettes?	Osake ya tabako o motte imasu ka?	お酒やタバコを持っていますか。
170	Are you carrying any food or plants?	Tabemono ya shokubutsu o motte imasu ka?	食べ物や植物を持っていますか。
171	What does this contain?	Kono nakami wa nan desu ka?	この中味は何ですか。
172	What is this medicine for?	Kore wa nan no kusuri desu ka?	これは何の薬ですか。

	ENGLISH	ROMANIZED JAPANESE	JAPANESE
173	Is this new or old?	Kore wa atarashii desu ka, furui desu ka?	これは新しいですか、古いですか。
174	Is this for your personal use?	Kore wa anata ga kojin de tsukau mono desu ka?	これはあなたが個人で使うものですか。
175	This is a prohibited article.	Kore wa mochikomi kinshihin desu.	これは持ち込み禁止品です。
176	I must confiscate this.	Kore wa bosshuu shimasu.	これは没収します。
177	You must pay customs duty on this.	Kore wa kanzei ga kakarimasu.	これは関税がかかります。
178	Go over there for the immigration check, please.	Nyuukoku shinsa wa achira desu.	入国審査はあちらです。

4 Departure and luggage

ENGLISH	ROMANIZED JAPANESE	JAPANESE
Departure	Shuppatsu	出発
Luggage/Baggage	Nimotsu	荷物
Checking-in	Chekkuin/Toojoo tetsuzuki	チェックイン、搭乗手続き
Check-in counter	Chekkuin kauntaa	チェックインカウンター
Airline ticket	Kookuuken	航空券
Passport	Pasupooto/Ryoken	パスポート、旅券
Seat allocation	Zaseki wariate	座席割当て
Smoking section	Kitsuenseki	喫煙席
Non-smoking section	Kin'enseki	禁煙席
Aircraft	Hikooki	飛行機
All	Zenbu	全部
Window seat	Madogawa no seki	窓側の席
Aisle seat	Tsuurogawa no seki	通路側の席
Separate seats	Betsubetsu no seki	別々の席
Seats next to each other	Tonariawase no seki	隣り合わせの席
Full seat	Manseki	満席

ENGLISH	ROMANIZED JAPANESE	JAPANESE
How many?	Ikutsu	いくつ
Scales	Hakari	計り
Hand luggage	Tenimotsu	手荷物
Cabin luggage	Kinai mochikomi nimotsu	機内持込み荷物
Overweight	Juuryoo chooka	重量超過
Luggage allowance	Muryoo tenimotsu kyoyooryoo	無料手荷物許容量
Excess charge	Chooka ryookin	超過料金
Contents	Nakami	中味
Fragile	Kowaremono	こわれ物
Flight number	Binmei	便名
Luggage claim tag	Nimotsu hikikaeshoo	荷物引換証
Customs clearance	Zeikan tetsuzuki	税関手続き
Duty-free goods	Menzeihin	免税品
Security check	Nimotsu kensa	荷物検査
Camera	Kamera	カメラ
Film	Fuirumu	フィルム

ENGLISH	ROMANIZED JAPANESE	JAPANESE
Boarding	Toojoo	搭乗
Boarding pass	Toojooken	搭乗券
Boarding gate	Geeto/Toojooguchi	ゲート、搭乗口
Now boarding	Toojoochuu	搭乗中
Departure lounge	Shuppatsu robii	出発ロビー
Departure time	Shuppatsu jikan	出発時間
Departure information board	Shuppatsu annaiban	出発案内板
Departure card	Shukkoku kaado	出国カード
Airport/Departure tax	Kuukoozei/Shukkokuzei	空港税，出国税
Cash	Genkin	現金
Local currency	Kono kuni no tsuuka	この国の通貨
Travellers cheque	Toraberaazu chekku	トラベラーズ　チェック
Child/Children	Kodomo	子供
Over 12 years old	Juunisai ijoo	12才以上
Economy class	Ekonomii kurasu	エコノミー　クラス
Exit seat	Iriguchi chikaku no seki	入口近くの席

ENGLISH	ROMANIZED JAPANESE	JAPANESE
Business class	Bijinesu kurasu	ビジネス　クラス
First class	Faasuto kurasu	ファースト　クラス
Dangerous goods	Kikenbutsu	危険物

	ENGLISH	ROMANIZED JAPANESE	JAPANESE
179	May I see your airline ticket?	Kookuuken o haiken shimasu.	航空券を拝見します。
180	The exit seat is not available.	Iriguchi chikaku no seki wa arimasen.	入口近くの席はありません。
181	Would you like to sit in a smoking section?	Kitsuenseki ga yoroshii desu ka?	喫煙席がよろしいですか。
182	Would you like to sit in a non-smoking section?	Kin'en seki ga ii desu ka?	禁煙席がいいですか。
183	It's all non-smoking on this flight.	Kono bin wa zenbu kin'en desu.	この便は全部禁煙です。
184	Would you like a window seat?	Madogawa no seki ga ii desu ka?	窓側の席がいいですか。
185	All the window seats are occupied.	Madogawa no seki wa fusagatte imasu.	窓側の席はふさがっています。
186	This is an aisle seat.	Tsuurogawa no seki desu.	通路側の席です。
187	You will be seated separately.	Betsubetsu no seki ni narimasu.	別々の席になります。
188	How many pieces of luggage have you got altogether?	Nimotsu wa zenbu de ikutsu desu ka?	荷物は全部でいくつですか。

44

	ENGLISH	ROMANIZED JAPANESE	JAPANESE
189	Please put the luggage on the scales.	Nimotsu o hakari no ue ni nosete kudasai.	荷物を計りの上に乗せてください。
190	Is that hand luggage?	Sore wa tenimotsu desu ka?	それは手荷物ですか。
191	Please limit your cabin luggage to one piece.	Kinai mochikomi tenimotsu wa ikko ni onegai shimasu.	機内持込手荷物は1個にお願いします。
192	You may carry that into the cabin.	Sore wa kinai ni mochikondemo ii desu.	それは機内に持ち込んでもいいです。
193	That is too big for carrying into the cabin.	Sore wa kinai mochikomi ni wa ooki sugimasu.	それは機内持ち込みには大きすぎます。
194	This is overweight.	Juuryoo chooka desu.	重量超過です。
195	Please reduce the content.	Nakami o herashite kudasai.	中味を減らして下さい。
196	You will have to pay $100 excess luggage charge.	Chooka ryookin to shite hyakudoru o oshiharai kudasai.	超過料金として100ドルをお支払い下さい。
197	I'll put a 'Fragile' sticker on this.	"Koware mono chuui" no sutekkaa o tsukemashoo.	"こわれ物注意"のステッカーを付けましょう。
198	We cannot put this luggage on your flight.	Kono nimotsu wa anata no bin ni maniaimasen.	この荷物はあなたの便に間に合いません。

	ENGLISH	ROMANIZED JAPANESE	JAPANESE
199	We will put it on the next flight.	Tsugi no bin ni nosemasu.	次の便に乗せます。
200	I have attached the claim tag to your ticket.	Nimotsu hikikaeshoo wa kookuuken ni tsukemashita.	荷物引換証は航空券に付けました。
201	What does this contain?	Nakami wa nan desu ka?	中味は何ですか。
202	This parcel has been cleared for customs at this counter.	Kono shinamono wa koko de zeikan tetsuzuki o shimashita.	この品物はここで税関手続きをしました。
203	Please show this at customs.	Kore o zeikan de misete kudasai.	これを税関で見せて下さい。
204	This parcel does not need a customs inspection.	Zeikan tetsuzuki o tooru hitsuyoo wa arimasen.	税関手続きを通る必要はありません。
205	This duty-free article has to go through customs inspection.	Sono menzeihin wa zeikan tetsuzuki o shite kudasai.	その免税品は税関手続きをして下さい。
206	Please stay outside of the rope.	Roopu yori naka ni hairanaide kudasai.	ロープより中に入らないで下さい。
207	Wait in the line.	Soko ni narande kudasai.	そこに並んで下さい。

	ENGLISH	ROMANIZED JAPANESE	JAPANESE
208	Please open your suitcase.	Suutsukeesu o akete kudasai.	スーツケースを開けて下さい。
209	Please let the camera go through too.	Kamera mo tooshite kudasai.	カメラも通して下さい。
210	Ordinary film won't be affected.	Futsuu no fuirumu wa kankoo shimasen.	普通のフィルムは感光しません。
211	This is a boarding pass.	Toojooken desu.	搭乗券です。
212	Please collect your boarding pass at the gate.	Toojooken wa geeto de owatashi shimasu.	搭乗券はゲートでお渡しします。
213	Boarding is at gate No.1.	Toojoo geeto wa ichiban desu.	搭乗ゲートは1番です。
214	Boarding time is 8 o'clock.	Toojoo kaishi wa hachiji desu.	搭乗開始は8時です。
215	The boarding gates are in that direction.	Toojoo geito wa achira desu.	搭乗ゲートはあちらです。
216	Please go down the escalator.	Esukareetaa o orite kudasai.	エスカレーターを降りて下さい。
217	Boarding has begun.	Toojoo ga hajimatte imasu.	搭乗が始まっています。

47

	ENGLISH	ROMANIZED JAPANESE	JAPANESE
218	Please hurry.	Isoide kudasai.	急いで下さい。
219	Have you filled in your departure card?	Shukkoku kaado wa kinyuu shimashita ka?	出国カードは記入しましたか。
220	The departure tax has already been paid.	Shukkokuzei wa shiharaizumi desu.	出国税は支払い済みです。
221	Please pay the tax at the counter over there.	Kuukoozei o achira no kauntaa de haratte kudasai.	空港税をあちらのカウンターで払って下さい。
222	Please pay in cash.	Genkin de onegai shimasu.	現金でお願いします。
223	How old is the child?	Okosan wa oikutsu desu ka?	お子さんはおいくつですか。
224	Persons over the age of 12 years must pay airport tax.	Juunisai ijoo no kata wa kuukoozei ga kakarimasu.	12才以上の方は空港税がかかります。
225	Are you carrying any dangerouse goods?	Kikenbutsu wa haitte imasen ka.	危険物は入っていませんか。
226	Baggage will be checked through to your final destination.	Nimotsu wa saishuu mokutekichi made tooshi de ikimasu.	荷物は最終目的地まで通しで行きます。
227	There will be a delay of fifty minutes.	Shuppatsu wa gojuppun okureru mikomi desu.	出発は50分遅れる見込みです。

5 Transit and airport

[1] See also 8. Train and coach trips — Part 1: Time schedule.

ENGLISH	ROMANIZED JAPANESE	JAPANESE
Transit	**Noritsugi/Toranjitto**	乗り継ぎ, トランジット
Airport	Kuukoo	空港
Aircraft	Hikooki	飛行機
Flight number	Binmei	便名
Connecting flight	Setsuzokubin	接続便
Seat allocation	Zaseki wariate	座席割当て
Seat number	Zaseki bangoo	座席番号
Luggage	Nimotsu	荷物
Transit time	Noritsugi jikan	乗り継ぎ時間
Locker	Rokkaa	ロッカー
Luggage cloakroom	Tenimotsu azukarisho	手荷物預り所
Domestic airline	Kokunaisen	国内線
International airline	Kokusaisen	国際線
Domestic flight	Kokunaibin	国内便
International flight	Kokusaibin	国際便
International airport	Kokusai kuukoo	国際空港
Counter	Kauntaa	カウンター

ENGLISH	ROMANIZED JAPANESE	JAPANESE
Checking-in	Toojoo tetsuzuki	搭 乗手続き
Bus for airport	Kuukoo iki no basu	空港行きのバス
Every 10 minutes	Juppun oki	10分おき
Airline ticket	Kookuuken	航空券
Free of charge	Muryoo	無料
Taxi	Takushii	タクシー
Local time	Genchi jikan	現地時間
Same time	Onaji jikan	同じ時間
Time difference	Jisa	時差
Late/Behind	Osoi	遅い
Early/Ahead	Hayai	早い
2 hours	Nijikan	2時間
Summer time	Natsu jikan	夏時間
Standard time	Hyoojun no jikan	標準の時間
Clock/Watch	Tokei	時計
2 a.m.	Gozen niji	午前2時
Bank	Ginkoo	銀行

ENGLISH	ROMANIZED JAPANESE	JAPANESE
Main entrance	Shoomen iriguchi	正面入口
Restaurant	Resutoran	レストラン
Upper floor	Ue no kai	上の階
Escalator	Esukareetaa	エスカレーター
Elevator	Erebeetaa	エレベーター
Information desk	An'naijo	案内所
First (ground) floor	Ikkai	1階
Paging	Yobidashi	呼び出し
Public telephone	Kooshuudenwa	公衆電話
Toilet	Toire/Otearai	トイレ、お手洗い
Post office	Yuubinkyoku	郵便局
Observation deck	Soogei dekki	送迎デッキ
Bound for city	Shinai iki	市内行き
Bus fare	Basu no ryookin	バスの料金
Taxi fare	Takushii ryookin	タクシー料金
End of bus line	Shuuten	終点

	ENGLISH	ROMANIZED JAPANESE	JAPANESE
228	Are you a transit passenger?	Noritsugi desu ka?	乗り継ぎですか。
229	You can go outside by showing this pass.	Kono ken o misereba soto ni deraremasu.	この券を見せれば外に出られます。
230	You will be boarding the same plane.	Onaji hikooki desu.	同じ飛行機です。
231	It's the same plane with a different flight number.	Onaji hikooki desu ga bin'mei ga kawarimasu.	同じ飛行機ですが、便名がかわります。
232	The connecting flight will depart at 4 o'clock.	Setsuzokubin wa yoji ni demasu.	接続便は4時に出ます。
233	There is sufficient time for transit.	Noritsugi jikan wa juubun arimasu.	乗り継ぎ時間は十分あります。
234	Please be careful as the transit time is rather tight.	Noritsugi jikan ga sukunai node ki o tsukete kudasai.	乗り継ぎ時間が少ないので気をつけて下さい。
235	Please take your luggage when you get off the plane.	Nimotsu o motte orite kudasai.	荷物を持って降りて下さい。
236	There are coin-operated lockers.	Koin rokkaa ga arimasu.	コインロッカーがあります。

53

	ENGLISH	ROMANIZED JAPANESE	JAPANESE
237	There is no cloakroom (in which to leave your luggage).	Tenimotsu azukarisho wa arimasen.	手荷物預り所はありません。
238	Please collect your luggage and go to the domestic airport.	Nimotsu o uketotte, kokunaisen kuukoo ni itte kudasai.	荷物を受け取って、国内線空港に行って下さい。
239	Your seat number will change.	Zaseki bangoo ga kawarimasu.	座席番号がかわります。
240	Please get off the plane and have your seat re-allocated.	Ichido orite, zaseki wariate tetsuzuki o shite kudasai.	一度降りて、座席割当て手続きをして下さい。
241	Please complete checking-in at the domestic flight counter.	Kokunaisen de toojoo tetsuzuki o shite kudasai.	国内線で搭乗手続きをして下さい。
242	The domestic flight counters are in that direction.	Kokunaisen kauntaa wa achira desu.	国内線カウンターはあちらです。
243	You cannot check in at this counter.	Kono kauntaa dewa chekkuin dekimasen.	このカウンターではチェックインできません。
244	You can check in here for domestic flights.	Koko de kokunaibin no chekkuin ga dekimasu.	ここで国内便のチェックインができます。

	ENGLISH	ROMANIZED JAPANESE	JAPANESE
245	There are both international and domestic services at this airport.	Kono kuukoo wa, kokusaisen to kokunaisen no ryoohoo ga arimasu.	この空港は、国際線と国内線の両方があります。
246	The international airport is located separately.	Kokusaisen no kuukoo wa betsu no tokoro ni arimasu.	国際線の空港は別のところにあります。
247	There is a bus service to the international airport.	Kokusai kuukoo iki no basu ga arimasu.	国際空港行きのバスがあります。
248	It takes 10 minutes by bus.	Basu de juppun kakarimasu.	バスで10分かかります。
249	There is a bus running every 20 minutes.	Basu wa nijuppun oki ni deteimasu.	バスは20分おきに出ています。
250	The ride is free if you show your airline ticket.	Kookuuken o misereba muryoo de noremasu.	航空券を見せれば無料で乗れます。
251	It would be quicker to go by taxi.	Takushii no hoo ga hayai deshoo.	タクシーの方が早いでしょう。
252	The local time is half-past 5.	Genchi jikan wa gojihan desu.	現地時間は5時半です。

	ENGLISH	ROMANIZED JAPANESE	JAPANESE
253	Paris and Berlin have the same time.	Pari to Berurin wa onaji jikan desu.	パリとベルリンは同じ時間です。
254	There is a 6 hour time difference.	Rokujikan no jisa ga arimasu.	6時間の時差があります。
255	Jakarta is behind us by 3 hours.	Jakaruta wa sanjikan okurete imasu.	ジャカルタは3時間遅れています。
256	New Zealand is ahead of us by 2 hours.	Nyuujiirando wa nijikan hayai desu.	ニュージーランドは2時間早いです。
257	We are on summer time now.	Ima, natsu jikan ni natte imasu.	今、夏時間になっています。
258	The time is one hour ahead of the standard time.	Hyoojun no jikan yori ichijikan susunde imasu.	標準の時間より1時間進んでいます。
259	Summer time will start tommorrow.	Asu kara natsu jikan ga hajimarimasu.	明日から夏時間が始まります。
260	Summer time will end tommorow.	Ashita, natsu jikan ga owarimasu.	明日、夏時間が終わります。

	ENGLISH	ROMANIZED JAPANESE	JAPANESE
261	Put your watch back one hour.	Jikan o ichijikan okurasete kudasai.	時間を1時間遅らせて下さい。
262	There is a bank near the front entrance.	Ginkoo wa shoomen iriguchi no chikaku ni arimasu.	銀行は正面入口の近くにあります。
263	The bank is open until 4 o'clock.	Ginkoo wa yoji made aite imasu.	銀行は4時まで開いています。
264	There is a restaurant on the upper floor.	Resutoran wa ue no kai ni arimasu.	レストランは上の階にあります。
265	There is a bar at the top of the escalator.	Esukareetaa o agatta tokoro ni baa ga arimasu.	エスカレーターを上がったところにバーがあります。
266	There is an information desk on the first (i.e. ground) floor.	Ikkai ni an'naijo ga arimasu.	1階に案内所があります。
267	There are Japanese-speaking staff at the information desk.	**An'naijo ni Nihongo o hanasu hito ga imasu.**	案内所に日本語を話す人がいます。
268	We do not accept any paging at the airport.	Kuukoo deno yobidashi wa shite orimasen.	空港での呼び出しはしておりません。

	ENGLISH	ROMANIZED JAPANESE	JAPANESE
269	There is a post office over there.	Yuubinkyoku wa achira ni arimasu.	郵便局はあちらにあります。
270	There is a bus going to the city.	Shinai ni iku renraku basu ga dete imasu.	市内に行く連絡バスが出ています。
271	It is 25 kilometres from the airport to the city.	Kuukoo kara shinai made nijuugokiro desu.	空港から市内まで25キロです。
272	It takes half-an-hour to the city.	Shinai made sanjuppun kakarimasu.	市内まで30分かかります。
273	The bus fare is $5.	Basu no ryookin wa godoru desu.	バスの料金は5ドルです。
274	The taxi fare will be about $18.	Takushii ryookin wa juuhachi doru gurai desu.	タクシー料金は18ドル位です。
275	The bus does not stop at hotels.	Basu wa hoteru ni tomarimasen.	バスはホテルに止まりません。
276	The last stop is the city terminal.	Shuuten wa shinai no taaminaru desu.	終点は市内のターミナルです。

6 Reservations and change of schedule

[1] See also 8. Train and coach trips – Part 1: Time schedule.
[2] See also 8. Train and coach trips – Part 1: Tickets.

ENGLISH	ROMANIZED JAPANESE	JAPANESE
Reservations	Yoyaku	予約
Alteration	Henkoo	変更
Direct flight	Chokkoobin	直行便
Every day	Mainichi	毎日
Timetable	Jikokuhyoo	時刻表
Flying time	Shoyoo jikan	所要時間
10 hours	Juujikan	10時間
Via ―	― keiyu	～経由
Transit	**Noritsugi/Toranjitto**	**乗り継ぎ，トランジット**
12 noon	Shoogo juuniji	正午12時
Departure	Shuppatsu	出発
Flight	**Bin/Furaito**	**便、フライト**
Vacant seat	Kuuseki	空席
Arrival	Toochaku	到着
6 a.m.	Gozen rokuji	午前6時
Meal on board	Kinaishoku	機内食
Lunch	Ranchi/Chuushoku	ランチ、昼食

ENGLISH	ROMANIZED JAPANESE	JAPANESE
Fare	Unchin	運賃
Contact telephone number	Renrakusaki	連絡先
Intended place of stay	Taizaisaki	滞在先
Telephone number	Denwa bangoo	電話番号
Schedule	Sukejuuru/Yotei	スケジュール、予定
Contact	Renraku	連絡
30 minutes before	Sanjuppun mae	30分前
Identification	Mibun shoomeisho	身分証明書
Driving licence	Jidoosha unten menkyoshoo	自動車運転免許証
Scheduled time	Yotei jikoku	予定時刻
Reconfirmation	Saikakunin	再確認
On the waiting list	Kuusekimachi	空席待ち
Name	Namae	名前
Surname	Myooji	名字
Spelling	Tsuzuri	つづり
Initial	Inisharu	イニシャル

Reservations and change of schedule

ENGLISH	ROMANIZED JAPANESE	JAPANESE
Airline ticket	Kookuuken	航空券
Group ticket	Dantai kippu	団体切符
The airline company that issued the ticket	Hakkoo kookuugaisha	発行航空会社
Endorsement	Uragaki	裏書き
Refund	Haraimodoshi	払い戻し
Cancel	Torikeshi/Kyanseru	取り消し、キャンセル
Invalid	Mukoo	無効
Delay	Okure	遅れ
Aircraft	Hikooki	飛行機
Out of order	Koshoo	故障
Departure information board	Shuppatsu an'naiban	出発案内板
Fog	Kiri	霧
Bad weather	Tenkoo ga warui	天候が悪い
Airport	Kuukoo	空港
Strike	Sutoraiki	ストライキ
Closed	Heisachuu	閉鎖中

	ENGLISH	ROMANIZED JAPANESE	JAPANESE
277	There is no direct flight.	Chokkoobin wa arimasen.	直行便はありません。
278	It flies every day.	Mainichi unkoo sarete imasu.	毎日運行されています。
279	The flying time is 10 hours.	Shoyoo jikan wa juujikan desu.	所要時間は10時間です。
280	It takes 9 hours by direct flight.	Chokkoobin de kujikan desu.	直行便で9時間です。
281	It is 15 hours flying via Hong Kong.	Honkon keiyu dato juugojikan desu.	ホンコン経由だと15時間です。
282	You change your flight at Manila.	Manira de noritsugi desu.	マニラで乗り継ぎです。
283	There is a flight leaving at 12 noon.	Shoogo juuniji hatsu no bin ga arimasu.	正午12時発の便があります。
284	There is a seat available on this flight.	Kono bin nara kuuseki ga arimasu.	この便なら空席があります。
285	You arrive at Bangkok at 6 a.m.	Bankokku toochaku wa gozen rokuji desu.	バンコック到着は午前6時です。

	ENGLISH	ROMANIZED JAPANESE	JAPANESE
286	There is a meal served on this flight.	Kono bin dewa kinaishoku ga arimasu.	この便では機内食があります。
287	Lunch will not be served on this flight.	Kono bin dewa ranchi wa demasen.	この便ではランチは出ません。
288	The air fare is $1200.	Kookuu unchin wa sen'nihyaku doru desu.	航空運賃は1200ドルです。
289	Where will you be staying?	Taizaisaki wa doko desu ka?	滞在先はどこですか。
290	Please give me a contact telephone number.	Renrakusaki no denwa bangoo o oshiete kudasai.	連絡先の電話番号を教えて下さい。
291	Please call us as soon as you know it.	Wakari shidai denwa shite kudasai.	分かり次第電話して下さい。
292	We'll contact you if there is a change of schedule.	Sukejuuru ni henkoo ga attara renraku shimasu.	スケジュールに変更があったら連絡します。
293	Please contact us on 654 8623.	Roku go yon no hachi roku ni san ni denwa shite kudasai.	6548623に電話して下さい。

	ENGLISH	ROMANIZED JAPANESE	JAPANESE
294	Please check in 30 minutes before the departure time.	Shuppatsu no sanjuppun mae made ni chekkuin shite kudasai.	出発の30分前までにチェックインして下さい。
295	Please show me some identification.	Mibun shoomeisho o misete kudasai.	身分証明書を見せて下さい。
296	A driving licence will be fine.	Jidoosha unten menkyoshoo de kekkoodesu.	自動車運転免許証で結構です。
297	Please reconfirm 72 hours before the scheduled departure time.	Shuppatsu yotei jikoku no nanajuunijikan mae made ni saikakunin shite kudasai.	出発予定時刻の72時間前までに再確認して下さい。
298	**You are still on the waiting list.**	Mada kuuseki machi desu.	まだ空席待ちです。
299	What is your name?	Onamae wa?	お名前は?
300	Please spell your name.	Onamae no tsuzuri o itte kudasai.	お名前のつづりを言って下さい。
301	Which one is your surname?	Myooji wa dochira desu ka?	名字はどちらですか。

	ENGLISH	ROMANIZED JAPANESE	JAPANESE
302	What is the initial of your first name?	Namae no inisharu wa nan desu ka?	名前のイニシアルは何ですか。
303	We cannot make any changes to this ticket.	Kono kookuuken wa henkoo dekimasen.	この航空券は変更できません。
304	We cannot make any changes to a group ticket.	Dantaiyoo no kippuu wa henkoo dekimasen.	団体用の切符は変更できません。
305	It has to be endorsed by the airline company that issued it.	Hakkoo kookuu gaisha no uragaki ga irimasu.	発行航空会社の裏書きが要ります。
306	There are no seats available in economy class.	Ekonomii kurasu dewa kuuseki wa arimasen.	エコノミークラスでは空席はありません。
307	I can get you a seat in first class.	Faasuto kurasu nara seki ga arimasu.	ファーストクラスなら席があります。
308	The balance of the fare is $400.	Sagaku wa yonhyakudoru desu.	差額は400ドルです。
309	We cannot refund you here.	Harai modoshi wa koko dewa dekimasen.	払い戻しはここでは出来ません。

	ENGLISH	ROMANIZED JAPANESE	JAPANESE
310	The airline company that issued the ticket will refund you.	Kookuuken hakkoo gaisha ga harai modoshimasu.	航空券発行会社が払い戻します。
311	Would you like to cancel this reservation?	Kono yoyaku wa torikeshimasu ka?	この予約は取り消しますか。
312	This ticket is invalid now.	Kono kippu wa mukoo ni narimasu.	この切符は無効になります。
313	The departure of your flight is delayed by 1 hour.	Kono bin no shuppatsu wa ichijikan okuremasu.	この便の出発は1時間遅れます。
314	This flight will not fly according to schedule.	Teikoku ni shuppatsu dekimasen.	定刻に出発できません。
315	The aircraft has to be repaired.	Hikooki no koshoo desu.	飛行機の故障です。
316	We hope you don't have to wait long.	Moo shibaraku omachi kudasai.	もうしばらくお待ち下さい。
317	I'm sorry to have kept you waiting.	Omatase shimashita.	お待たせしました。

	ENGLISH	ROMANIZED JAPANESE	JAPANESE
318	Please check the time with the departure information board.	Shuppatsu an'naiban de jikan o tashikamete kudasai.	出発案内板で時間を確かめて下さい。
319	Due to bad weather there are no outgoing flights.	Tenkoo ga warui tame hikooki wa demasen.	天候が悪いため飛行機は出ません。
320	Due to an industrial dispute, Sydney airport is closed.	Suto no tame Shidonii kuukoo wa heisachuu desu.	ストのためシドニー空港は閉鎖中です。
321	This flight has been cancelled.	Kono bin wa kyanseru desu.	この便はキャンセルです。
322	All today's flights have been cancelled.	Kyoo no bin wa zenbu kyanseru desu.	今日の便は全部キャンセルです。
323	At the moment we cannot predict when you will be able to leave.	Ima no tokoro, itsu shuppatsu dekiru ka wakarimasen.	今のところ、いつ出発できるか分かりません。
324	Would you like me to try another airline?	Hoka no kookuu gaisha o shirabete mimashoo ka?	外の航空会社を調べてみましょうか。
325	I have booked you on this flight.	Kono bin ni yoyaku shimashita.	この便に予約しました。

7 At the bank

69

ENGLISH	ROMANIZED JAPANESE	JAPANESE
Bank	Ginkoo	銀行
Automatic teller machine	Kyasshu disupensaa	キャッシュ　ディスペンサー
In the afternoon	Yuugata	夕方
Weekend	Shuumatsu	週末
Trading hours	Eigyoo jikan	営業時間
Teller	Madoguchi	窓口
Queue	Retsu	列
No. 5	Goban	5番
Money	Okane	お金
Australian dollars	Oosutoraria doru	オーストラリアドル
American dollars	Amerika doru/Bei doru	アメリカドル、米ドル
Japanese yen	Nihon en	日本円
Local currency	Genchi tsuuka	現地通貨
$300	Sanbyaku doru	300ドル
Exchange of money	Ryoogae	両替
Up to ～	～ made	～まで
Limit	Seigen	制限

ENGLISH	ROMANIZED JAPANESE	JAPANESE
Passport	Pasupooto/Ryoken	パスポート、旅券
Flight name	Binmei	便名
Arrival	Toochaku	到着
Exchange (office)	Ryoogaejo	両替所
Exchange rate	Kookan reeto	交換レート
Coins	Kooka/Koin	硬貨, コイン
Notes	Shihei/Osatsu	紙弊、お札
Commemorative coins	Kinen kooka	記念硬貨
Small change	Kozeni	小銭
Cash	Genkin	現金
20 cents	Nijussento	20セント
50 cent coin	Gojussento kooka	50セント硬貨
$10	Juudoru	10ドル
$100 note	Hyakudoru shihei	100ドル紙弊
Address	Juusho	住所
Name	Namae	名前
Signature	Shomei/Sain	署名、サイン

ENGLISH	ROMANIZED JAPANESE	JAPANESE
Passport number	Ryoken/Pasupooto bangoo	旅券番号、パスポート番号
Handling charge	Tesuuryoo	手数料
Travellers cheque	Toraberaazu chekku	トラベラーズ　チェック
Issue	Hakkoo	発行
Japanese bank	Nihon no ginkoo	日本の銀行
Branch	Shiten	支店
Lost	Funshitsu	紛失
Theft	Toonan	盗難
Cancel (e.g. credit card)	Mukoo ni suru	無効にする
Measures (steps)	Sochi	措置
Re-issue	Saihakkoo	再発行
Application form	Shinsei yooshi	申請用紙
Within 3 days	Mikka inai	3日以内
Procedure	Tetsuzuki	手続き
Telephone number for contact	Renrakusaki denwa bangoo	連絡先電話番号
Place of stay	Taizaisaki	滞在先

	ENGLISH	ROMANIZED JAPANESE	JAPANESE
326	The bank is on the first (i.e. ground) floor.	Ginkoo wa ikkai ni arimasu.	銀行は1階にあります。
327	The bank will open at 9 o'clock.	Ginkoo wa kuji ni akimasu.	銀行は9時に開きます。
328	The bank is closed now.	Ginkoo wa ima shimatte imasu.	銀行は今閉まっています。
329	The bank will be open until 4 p.m.	Yuugata yoji made aite imasu.	夕方4時まで開いています。
330	Banks do not trade on the weekend.	Ginkoo wa shuumatsu wa eigyoo shite imasen.	銀行は週末は営業していません。
331	Please wait there in the queue for the teller there.	Achira no madoguchi ni narande kudasai.	あちらの窓口に並んで下さい。
332	You can go to any teller.	Dono madoguchi demo ii desu.	どの窓口でもいいです。
333	Please go to the teller when your name is called.	Namae o yobaretara madoguchi ni itte kudasai.	名前を呼ばれたら窓口に行って下さい。

	ENGLISH	ROMANIZED JAPANESE	JAPANESE
334	Please collect it at the No.5 teller.	Goban no madoguchi de uketotte kudasai.	5番の窓口で受け取って下さい。
335	Please change your money into Singapore dollars.	Shingapooru doru ni kaete kudasai.	シンガポールドルに換えて下さい。
336	American dollars cannot be used here.	Amerika doru wa kokodewa tsuuyoo shimasen.	アメリカドルはここでは通用しません。
337	You can change up to $300.	Sanbyakudoru made ryoogae dekimasu.	300ドルまで両替できます。
338	May I see your passport?	Pasupooto o misete kudasai.	パスポートを見せて下さい。
339	On which flight did you arrive?	Dono bin de toochaku shinmashita ka?	どの便で到着しましたか。
340	This is today's exchange rate.	**Kyoo no kookan reeto wa kore desu.**	今日の交換レートはこれです。
341	One Australian dollar is equivalent to 100 yen.	Oosutoraria no ichidoru ni taishite hyakuen desu.	オーストラリアの1ドルに対して100円です。
342	Into which currency do you want to change?	Dono kuni no tsuuka ni kaetai no desu ka?	どの国の通貨にかえたいのですか。

	ENGLISH	ROMANIZED JAPANESE	JAPANESE
343	You cannot exchange the coins.	Kooka wa ryoogae dekimasen.	硬貨は両替できません。
344	We cannot cash this cheque.	Kono kogitte wa genkinka dekimasen.	この小切手は現金化できません。
345	We don't have any $20 notes.	Nijuudoru no shihei ga arimasen.	20ドルの紙弊がありません。
346	Are $100 notes all right?	Hyakudoru shihei demo ii desu ka?	100ドル紙弊でもいいですか。
347	We don't have any 50 cent coins.	Gojussento kooka wa arimasen.	50セント硬貨はありません。
348	Please write your name and address.	Juusho to namae o kaite kudasai.	住所と名前を書いて下さい。
349	Please sign here.	Koko ni shomei shite kudasai.	ここに署名して下さい。
350	You can withdraw cash by card.	Kaado de genkin ga hikidasemasu.	カードで現金が引き出せます。
351	Please write your passport number.	Pasupooto bangoo o kaite kudasai.	パスポート番号を書いて下さい。

	ENGLISH	ROMANIZED JAPANESE	JAPANESE
352	The handling charge is $5.	Tesuuryoo wa godoru desu.	手数料は5ドルです。
353	When did you lose it?	Itsu nakushimashita ka?	いつなくしましたか。
354	Which bank issued the cheque?	Doko ga hakkoo shita kogitte desu ka?	どこが発行した小切手ですか。
355	It is not handled by this bank.	Kono ginkoo dewa atsukatte imasen.	この銀行では扱っていません。
356	We will take measures to cancel it.	Mukoo ni suru sochi o torimasu.	無効にする措置を取ります。
357	Re-issue takes about 3 days.	Saihakkoo niwa mikka gurai kakarimasu.	再発行には3日位かかります。
358	Please fill in the application form for re-issue.	Saihakkooyoo no shinsei yooshi ni kinyuu shite kudasai.	再発行用の申請用紙に記入して下さい。
359	Where are you staying?	Taizaisaki wa dochira desu ka?	滞在先はどちらですか。
360	You can collect it the day after tomorrow.	Asatte tori ni kite kudasai.	あさって取りに来て下さい。

8 Train and coach trips – Part 1

[1] See also 6. Reservations and change of schedule: Flight information, Reservations.
[2] See also 4. Departure and luggage: Checking-in.

ENGLISH	ROMANIZED JAPANESE	JAPANESE
Railway	Tetsudoo	鉄道
Train	Ressha/Densha	列車、電車
Long-distance train	Chookyori ressha	長距離列車
Local train	Koogai densha	郊外電車
Underground railway	Chikatetsu	地下鉄
Tram	Shiden	市電
Station	Eki	駅
Coach/Bus	Basu	バス
Coach terminal	Basu hacchakujo	バス発着所
Ship/Boat	Fune	船
Departure	Shuppatsu	出発
Arrival	Toochaku	到着
Every — hour(s)	— jikan oki	～時間おき
2 services (vehicle)	Nibin	2便
First-class seat	Ittooseki	1等席
Economy-class (carriage)	Nitooseki	2等席
Passenger	Jookyaku	乗客

ENGLISH	ROMANIZED JAPANESE	JAPANESE
Dining car	Shokudoosha	食堂車
Sleeping car	Shindaisha	寝台車
Air-conditioned	Reidanboo tsuki	冷暖房付き
For 1 person	Hitoriyoo	1人用
Shared (public)	Kyooyoo	共用
Fare/Charge/Tariff	Ryookin/Unchin	料金、運賃
Additional charge	Betsuryookin	別料金
Ticket	Kippu/Ken	切符、券
Voucher	Kuupon	クーポン
Reserved-seat ticket	Shiteiseki ken	指定席券
Round-trip ticket/Pass	Shuuyuu ken/Pasu	周遊券、パス
Distance	Kyori	距離
Unlimited/No restriction	Museigen	無制限
Discount	Waribiki	割引き
First day of use	Shiyookaishibi	使用開始日
For the period of — days	— nichikan	〜日間
Effective/Valid	Yuukoo	有効

ENGLISH	ROMANIZED JAPANESE	JAPANESE
Invalid	Mukoo	無効
(Train/Bus) conductor	Shashoo	車掌
Attendant	Kakari' in	係員
Adult fare	Otona ryookin	大人料金
Children's fare	Kodomo ryookin	子供料金
Under 12 years old	Juunisai ika	12才以下
Single/One-way	Katamichi	片道
Return	Oofuku	往復
All-day ticket	Ichinichi yuukoo kippu	1日有効切符
Luggage	Nimotsu	荷物
Luggage for checking-in	Azukeru nimotsu	預ける荷物
Limit	Seigen	制限
Up to — kilograms	— kiro made	～キロまで
Free of charge	Muryoo	無料
Confirmation/Checking	Kakunin	確認
Boot (vehicle)	Toranku	トランク

	ENGLISH	ROMANIZED JAPANESE	JAPANESE
361	It will depart at 10 o'clock in the morning.	Asa juuji ni shuppatsu shimasu.	朝10時に出発します。
362	It will arrive at 6 o'clock in the afternoon.	Gogo rokuji ni toochaku shimasu.	午後6時に到着します。
363	It leaves every hour.	Ichijikan oki ni dete imasu.	1時間おきに出ています。
364	It runs every day.	Mainichi unkoo sarete imasu.	毎日運行されています。
365	There are 2 (flights/buses/ ships, etc) a day.	Ichinichi ni nibin arimasu.	1日に2便あります。
366	They are all first-class seats.	Zenbu ittooseki desu.	全部1等席です。
367	The economy-class carriages are put on to the train at the weekend.	Shuumatsu niwa nitoosha ga renketsu saremasu.	週末には2等車が連結され ます。
368	The first-class passengers can use the lounge facilities.	Ittoo jookyaku wa raunji o riyoo dekimasu.	1等乗客は、ラウンジを利 用できます。
369	It is air-conditioned.	Reidanboo ga tsuite imasu.	冷暖房がついています。

	ENGLISH	ROMANIZED JAPANESE	JAPANESE
370	There is no dining car.	Shokudoosha wa tsuite imasen.	食堂車はついていません。
371	There is a public shower.	Shawaa wa kyoodoo desu.	シャワーは共同です。
372	There are individual sleeping compartments.	Hitoriyoo no shindaisha ga arimasu.	1人用の寝台車があります。
373	All the sleeping compartments are shared by 2 persons.	Shindaisha wa zenbu futariyoo desu.	寝台車は全部2人用です。
374	There is an extra charge for a sleeping compartment.	Shindai ryookin wa betsu ryookin desu.	寝台料金は別料金です。
375	The ticket for your seat also allows you to use a sleeping compartment.	Zaseki no yoyaku de shindaisha ga tsukaemasu.	座席の予約で寝台車が使えます。
376	You need a reserved-seat ticket.	Shiteiseki ken ga irimasu.	指定席券がいります。
377	There is a pass which allows you to travel for an unlimited distance.	Kyori museigen no shuuyuu ken ga arimasu.	距離無制限の周遊券があります。

	ENGLISH	ROMANIZED JAPANESE	JAPANESE
378	This ticket can be used for railways, suburban trains, buses and subways.	Kono kippu wa tetsudoo, koogai densha, basu, chikatetsu ni tsukaemasu.	この切符は、鉄道、郊外電車、バス、地下鉄に使えます。
379	It's not applicable for ship travel.	Fune niwa tsukaemasen.	船には使えません。
380	The discount rate is 20 per cent.	Waribikiritsu wa nijuppaasento desu.	割引き率は、20パーセントです。
381	It is valid for 60 days from the day you begin to use it.	Shiyoo kaishibi kara rokujuunichikan yuukoo desu.	使用開始日から60日間有効です。
382	This ticket is no longer valid.	Kono kippu wa moo mukoo desu.	この切符はもう無効です。
383	This is a book of vouchers.	Kore wa kuupon desu.	これはクーポンです。
384	An adult single fare is $10.	Otona ryookin wa katamichi juudoru desu.	大人料金は、片道10ドルです。
385	There is a discount on the return fare.	Oofuku ryookin wa waribiki ga arimasu.	往復料金は割引きがあります。

	ENGLISH	ROMANIZED JAPANESE	JAPANESE
386	Under 12 years old is children's fare.	Juunisai ika wa kodomo ryookin desu.	12才以下は子供料金です。
387	An all-day ticket is $5.	Ichinichi yuukoo kippu wa godoru desu.	一日有効切符は5ドルです。
388	This ticket allows you to have as many rides as you like (e.g. at Luna Park).	Kono ken de nankai demo norimono ni noremasu.	この券で何回でも乗り物に乗れます。
389	Please buy a separate entrance ticket here.	Koko no nyuujoo ken wa betsu ni katte kudasai.	ここの入場券は別に買って下さい。
390	Luggage is limited to 3 pieces.	Nimotsu wa sanko ga seigen desu.	荷物は3個が制限です。
391	Luggage is free of charge up to 80 kilograms.	Nimotsu wa hachijukkiro made muryoo desu.	荷物は80キロまで無料です。
392	Would you like to check in this luggage?	Kono nimotsu wa azukemasu ka?	この荷物は預けますか。
393	There are no porters.	Pootaa wa imasen.	ポーターはいません。

	ENGLISH	ROMANIZED JAPANESE	JAPANESE
394	Please get on board after checking your own luggage.	Jibun no nimotsu o kakunin shite kara notte kudasai.	自分の荷物を確認してから乗って下さい。
395	I'll put that luggage in the boot.	Sono nimotsu wa toranku ni iremashoo.	その荷物はトランクに入れましょう。

9 Train and coach trips – Part 2

[1] See also 2. On the plane: Seating.
     4. Departure and luggage: Seat allocation.
[2] See also 11. Sightseeing – Part 2: Greetings.
[3] See also 2. On the plane: Discomfort.
[4] See also 6. Reservations and change of schedule: Flight delay.

ENGLISH	ROMANIZED JAPANESE	JAPANESE
Seat allocation	Zaseki wariate	座席割当て
Window seat	Madogawa no seki	窓側の席
Front seats	Mae no hoo no seki	前の方の席
Back seats	Ushiro no hoo no seki	後ろの方の席
Driver/Coach captain	Untenshu	運転手
On the way	Tochuu	途中
— times	— kai	〜回
Stop/Rest	Kyuukei	休けい
As far as —	— made	〜まで
— minutes	— pun/— fun	〜分
Not feeling well	Kibun ga warui	気分が悪い
Restaurant	Resutoran	レストラン
Meals	Shokuji	食事
Number	Bangoo	番号
Parking	Chuusha	駐車
At what time?	Nanji ni	何時に
Which hotel?	Dono hoteru	どのホテル

ENGLISH	ROMANIZED JAPANESE	JAPANESE
Things left behind	Wasuremono	忘れ物
Slippery	Suberiyasui	すべりやすい
Cold	Samui	寒い
Hot	Atsui	暑い
Heater	Danboo	暖房
Cooler	Reiboo	冷房
Air conditioning	Eakon	エアコン
Music	Ongaku	音楽
Tape	Teepu	テープ
Video	Bideo	ビデオ
Button	Botan	ボタン
(Operated by hand) manual	Shudooshiki	手動式
Rubbish	Gomi	ごみ
Drinking water	Nomimizu	飲み水
On the right side	Migigawa	右側
On the left side	Hidarigawa	左側
Entrance	Iriguchi	入口

ENGLISH	ROMANIZED JAPANESE	JAPANESE
Exit	Deguchi	出口
Emergency exit	Hijyooguchi	非常口
Toilet	Toire/Otearai	トイレ、お手洗い
Mechanical trouble	Koshoo	故障
Accident	Jiko	事故
Replacement coach	Kawari no basu	代りのバス
Coach/Bus company	Basu gaisha	バス会社
Bound for —	— iki	〜行き
Platform No. —	— bansen	〜番線
— Station	— eki	〜駅
Next —	Tsugi no —	次の〜
Delay	Okure	遅れ
Express	Kyuukoo	急行
Terminus	Shuuten	終点
Change (bus, train, etc)	Norikae	乗りかえ
Carriage/Car	Sharyoo	車輌

	ENGLISH	ROMANIZED JAPANESE	JAPANESE
396	The seat allocation will be done at check-in time.	Zaseki wariate wa, chekkuin no toki ni shimasu.	座席割当ては、チェックインの時にします。
397	Would you like a window seat?	Madogawa no seki ga ii desu ka?	窓側の席がいいですか。
398	The seats towards the front are occupied.	Mae no hoo no seki wa fusagatte imasu.	前の方の席はふさがっています。
399	The seats in the back are smoking seats.	Ushiro no hoo no seki wa kitsuen seki desu.	後ろの方の席は喫煙席です。
400	On board, please.	Doozo notte kudasai.	どうぞ、乗って下さい。
401	We'll have 2 stops on the way.	Tochuu nikai kyuukei shimasu.	途中2回休けいします。
402	We won't stop until the hotel.	Hoteru made tomarimasen.	ホテルまで止まりません。
403	If anyone doesn't feel well on the way, please let me know.	Tochuu kibun ga warui hito wa itte kudasai.	途中気分が悪い人は言って下さい。
404	We'll stop here for half an hour.	Koko de sanjuppun kyuukei shimasu.	ここで30分休けいします。

	ENGLISH	ROMANIZED JAPANESE	JAPANESE
405	You can have a meal in that restaurant.	Ano resutoran de shokuji ga dekimasu.	あのレストランで食事ができます。
406	Please return to the coach by 2 o'clock.	Niji made ni basu ni modotte kudasai.	2時までにバスに戻って下さい。
407	Your coach will remain here.	Basu wa koko ni tomatte imasu.	バスはここに止まっています。
408	I'm not allowed to park here.	Koko ni chuusha dekimasen.	ここに駐車できません。
409	At what time do you want me to come back here?	Nanji ni koko ni modotte kimashoo ka?	何時にここに戻って来ましょうか。
410	You'll arrive at the hotel in 10 minutes.	Hoteru made ato juppun desu.	ホテルまであと10分です。
411	Which hotel are you staying at?	Dochira no hoteru ni otomari desu ka?	どちらのホテルにお泊りですか。
412	Please do not leave anything behind as you get off.	Wasuremono o shinaiyoo ni onegai shimasu.	忘れ物をしないようにお願いします。
413	Shall I put the heater on?	Danboo o iremashoo ka?	暖房を入れましょうか。

	ENGLISH	ROMANIZED JAPANESE	JAPANESE
414	Do you want me to turn off the cooler?	Reiboo o tomemashoo ka?	冷房を止めましょうか。
415	Is the air conditioning right for you?	Eakon wa choodo ii desu ka?	エアコンは丁度いいですか。
416	Do you want me to open the window a bit?	Mado o sukoshi akemashoo ka?	窓を少し開けましょうか。
417	Do you want me to stop for a short rest?	Sukoshi yasumimashoo ka?	少し休みましょうか。
418	Would you like to listen to some music on the tape?	Ongaku no teepu o kakemashoo ka?	音楽のテープをかけましょうか。
419	I can stop the car (bus) soon.	Moosugu tomeraremasu.	もうすぐ止められます。
420	Please book your breakfast now.	Ima, chooshoku no yoyaku o shite kudasai.	今、朝食の予約をして下さい。
421	The middle carriage is the dining car.	Shokudoosha wa man'naka no sharyoo desu.	食堂車は真中の車輌です。
422	Please push this button to call the attendant.	Kakari no hito o yobu niwa, kono botan o oshite kudasai.	係の人を呼ぶには、このボタンを押して下さい。

	ENGLISH	ROMANIZED JAPANESE	JAPANESE
423	Trains for Melbourne leave from Platform No. 5.	Meruborun iki wa gobansen desu.	メルボルン行きは5番線です。
424	The 'Aurora' is delayed.	Oororagoo wa okurete imasu.	オーロラ号は遅れています。
425	I'll let you know where you should get off.	Oriru tokoro wa oshiete agemashoo.	降りるところは教えてあげましょう。
426	The toilet is out of order and cannot be used.	Toire wa koshoochuu de tsukaemasen.	トイレは故障中で使えません。
427	I have some mechanical trouble with the car (bus).	Koshoo shimashita.	故障しました。
428	It will take about 2 hours to have it fixed.	Nijikan kurai de naorimasu.	2時間位で直ります。
429	I have radioed for another coach.	Kawari no basu o musen de tehai shimashita.	代りのバスを無線で手配しました。
430	A replacement coach will come by the time you finish your meal.	Shokuji ga owaru made ni kawari no basu ga kimasu.	食事が終わるまでに代りのバスが来ます。

10 Sightseeing – Part 1

[1] See also 8. Train and coach trips: Time schedule.
    19. Climate and clothing.
[2] See also 8. Train and coach trips: Tickets.

ENGLISH	ROMANIZED JAPANESE	JAPANESE
Sightseeing	Kankoo	観光
Map	Chizu	地図
You are here.	Genzaichi	現在置
Near	Chikai	近い
Far	Tooi	遠い
North	Kita	北
Direction/Towards	Hoogaku	方角
Distance	Kyori	距離
ー Kilometres	ー kiro	～キロ
About ー minutes	ー pun gurai	～分位
Street	Toori	通り
Corner	kado	角
On the right side	Migigawa	右側
On the left side	Hidarigawa	左側
In the middle	Man'naka	まん中
A set of traffic lights	Shingoo	信号
Intersection	Koosaten	交差点

ENGLISH	ROMANIZED JAPANESE	JAPANESE
Straight (ahead)	Massugu	まっすぐ
Opposite side	Hantaigawa	反対側
Plaza/Square	Hiroba	広場
Busy section of the city	Hankagai	繁華街
Big building	Ookina tatemono	大きな建物
Station	Eki	駅
International driving licence	Kokusai unten menkyoshoo	国際運転免許証
Over 20 years old	Nijussai ijoo	20才以上
Sightseeing coach service	Teiki kankoo basu	定期観光バス
Guide	Gaido	ガイド
Japanese-speaking guide	Nihongo gaido	日本語ガイド
Full-day tour	Ichinichi tsuaa	1日ツァー
Half-day tour	Han'nichi tsuaa	半日ツァー
Afternoon tour	Gogo no tsuaa	午後のツァー
City area	Shinai	市内
City-sights tour	Shinai kankoo	市内観光
Suburbs	Koogai	郊外

ENGLISH	ROMANIZED JAPANESE	JAPANESE
Country (as against city)	Inaka	田舎
Mountains	Yama	山
Sea/Beach	Umi	海
Beach/Coast	Kaigan	海岸
On the way	Tochuu	途中
Beautiful scenery	Kireina keshiki	きれいな景色
Cost of tour	Tsuaa ryookin	ツアー料金
Evening meal included	Yuushoku tsuki	夕食付き
Additional charge	Betsu ryookin	別料金
Reservations	Yoyaku	予約
Booking card	Mooshikomi ken	申込み券
Departure from hotel	Hoteru hatsu	ホテル発
Outside the hotel	Hoteru no soto	ホテルの外
Entrance	Iriguchi	入口
Lobby	Robii	ロビー
Passenger terminal	**Taaminaru**	**ターミナル**

	ENGLISH	ROMANIZED JAPANESE	JAPANESE
431	It's 15 kilometres from the city.	Shinai kara juugokiro desu.	市内から15キロです。
432	It's here on this map.	Kono chizu de koko desu.	この地図でここです。
433	It's towards the west.	Nishi no hoogaku desu.	西の方角です。
434	It will take about 2 hours driving.	Kuruma de nijikan gurai kakarimasu.	車で2時間位かかります。
435	You will drive through some beautiful scenery on the way.	Tochuu keshiki no ii tokoro o toorimasu.	途中景色のいい所を通ります。
436	North is that way.	Kita wa achira desu.	北はあちらです。
437	You are here on this map.	**Kono chizu de genzaichi wa koko desu.**	**この地図で現在置はここです。**
438	It will take about 20 minutes walking.	Aruite nijuppun kurai desu.	歩いて20分位です。
439	It's in this street.	Kono toori ni arimasu.	この通りにあります。
440	There's a department store on this corner.	Kono kado ni depaato ga arimasu.	この角にデパートがあります。

99

	ENGLISH	ROMANIZED JAPANESE	JAPANESE
441	Turn to the left at the third set of traffic lights.	Mittsume no shingoo o migi ni magatte kudasai.	3つ目の信号を右に曲って下さい。
442	It's near this intersection.	Kono koosaten no chikaku desu.	この交差点の近くです。
443	This section is the busiest part of the city.	Kono atari wa shinai no ichiban nigiyakana tokoro desu.	このあたりは市内の一番にぎやかな所です。
444	There are many offices around here.	Kono atari wa ofisugai desu.	このあたりはオフィス街です。
445	You cannot book a rented car here.	Rentakaa wa koko de wa mooshikomemasen.	レンタカーはここでは申し込めません。
446	Have you got an international driving licence?	Kokusai unten menkyoshoo o motte imasu ka?	国際運転免許証を持っていますか。
447	Are you over 20 years of age?	Anata wa nijussai ijoo desu ka?	あなたは20才以上ですか。
448	You are not allowed to drive a rented car unless you are over 20 years old.	Nijussai ijoo de nai to rentakaa no unten wa yurusaremasen.	20才以上でないとレンタカーの運転は許されません。

449	Joining a coach tour will be the best way.	Teiki kankoo basu ga ichiban benri desu.	定期観光バスが一番便利です。
450	There is a Japanese-speaking guide on this tour.	Kono tsuaa niwa, nihongo gaido ga tsukimasu.	このツアーには、日本語ガイドがつきます。
451	This tour is available every day.	Kono tsuaa wa mainichi dete imasu.	このツアーは毎日出ています。
452	There is no tour going to that island.	Sono shima ni iku tsuaa wa arimasen.	その島に行くツアーはありません。
453	There is some walking included in this tour.	**Kono tsuaa dewa sukoshi aruku tokoro ga arimasu.**	**このツアーでは少し歩く所があります。**
454	It's a full-day tour.	Ichinichi no tsuaa desu.	1日のツアーです。
455	This tour will take you to the mountains.	Kono tsuaa wa yama ni ikimasu.	このツアーは山に行きます。
456	You'll drive along some beautiful coastline.	Subarashii kaigan o toorimasu.	すばらしい海岸を通ります。
457	The cost is $120 per person.	Ryookin wa hitori hyakunijuudoru desu.	料金は1人120ドルです。

	ENGLISH	ROMANIZED JAPANESE	JAPANESE
458	Lunch is not included in the tour cost.	Ranchi wa tsuaa ryookin ni fukumarete imasen.	ランチはツアー料金に含まれていません。
459	You'll get back to the city at about 6 o'clock.	Rokuji goro shinai ni modorimasu.	6時頃市内に戻ります。
460	Shall I book for you?	Yoyaku shimashoo ka?	予約しましょうか。
461	Would you write your name, please?	Onamae o kaite kudasai.	お名前を書いて下さい。
462	I have booked you on this tour.	Kono tsuaa ni mooshikomi-mashita.	このツアーに申し込みました。
463	Please pay for the tour on the coach.	Ryookin wa basu no nake de haratte kudasai.	料金はバスの中で払って下さい。
464	The bus will leave your hotel at 9 o'clock tomorrow.	Basu wa ashita kuji ni hoteru hatsu desu.	バスはあした9時にホテル発です。
465	A Greyhound bus will pick you up at the hotel.	Gureihaundo to yuu basu ga hoteru ni mukae ni kimasu.	グレイハウンドというバスがホテルに迎えに来ます。
466	Please wait outside the hotel entrance.	Hoteru no iriguchi no soto de matte ite kudasai.	ホテルの入口の外で待っていて下さい。

	ENGLISH	ROMANIZED JAPANESE	JAPANESE
467	Is this a Nippon Tour group?	Nippon tsuaa no guruupu desu ka?	ニッポンツアーのグループ ですか。
468	I am your driver/chauffeur.	Watashi wa minasan no untenshu desu.	私は皆さんの運転手です。
469	The guide doesn't seem to have arrived.	Gaido ga kite inai yoo desu.	ガイドが来ていないようで す。
470	Your guide is waiting at the restaurant.	Gaido wa resutoran de matte imasu.	ガイドはレストランで待っ ています。
471	I'll make a telephone call to the tour company.	Ryokoo gaisha ni denwa shimasu.	旅行会社に電話します。
472	Please speak in Japanese.	Nihongo de hanashite kudasai.	日本語で話して下さい。
473	I'll take you to the city.	Watashi ga shinai made otsure shimasu.	私が市内までお連れします。
474	I'm just going to bring the car here.	Ima, kuruma o kochira ni mawashimasu.	今、車をこちらに回します。
475	Please wait here.	Koko de matte ite kudasai.	ここで待っていて下さい。

	ENGLISH	ROMANIZED JAPANESE	JAPANESE
476	We'll have to leave as time is running out.	Jikan ga arimasen kara shuppatsu shimashoo.	時間がありませんから出発しましょう。
477	Have you got all the luggage?	Nimotsu wa zenbu arimasu ka?	荷物は全部ありますか。
478	I'll help you with checking in.	Watashi ga chekkuin no otetsudai o shimasu.	私がチェックインのお手伝いをします。
479	Everything is all right. Don't worry.	Daijoobu desu. Goanshin kudasai.	大丈夫です。ご安心下さい。

Sightseeing – Part 2

ENGLISH	ROMANIZED JAPANESE	JAPANESE
Time to meet	Shuugoo jikan	集合時間
Place to meet	Shuugoo basho	集合場所
The largest in the world	Sekai de ichiban ookii	世界で一番大きい
The tallest in the Southern Hemisphere	Minamihankyuu de ichiban takai	南半球で一番高い
The newest in Australia	Oosutoraria de ichiban atarashii	オーストラリアで一番新しい
The oldest in this country	Kono kuni de ichiban furui	この国で一番古い
Famous	Yuumeina	有名な
Building	Tatemono	建物
Church/Cathedral	Kyookai	教会
Parliament House	Gijidoo	議事堂
Theatre	Gekijoo	劇場
Art gallery	Bijutsukan	美術館
Stadium	Sutajiamu	スタジアム
Park/Public garden	Kooen	公園
Animal/Fauna	Doobutsu	動物

ENGLISH	ROMANIZED JAPANESE	JAPANESE
Zoo/Animal Sanctuary	Doobutsuen	動物園
Plant/Flora	Shokubutsu	植物
Botanical Gardens	Shokubutsuen	植物園
Bird	Tori	鳥
Wild animals	Yasei doobutsu	野生動物
Wild birds	Yachoo	野鳥
Feed (animal and bird)/Bait	Esa	餌
Tree	Ki	木
Flower	Hana	花
Farm	Noojoo	農場
Sheep dog	Bokuyooken	牧羊犬
Shearing	Yoomoogari	羊毛刈り
Winery	Wainarii	ワイナリー
Aquarium	Suizokukan	水族館
Fish	Sakana	魚
Shell	Kai	貝

ENGLISH	ROMANIZED JAPANESE	JAPANESE
Male (animals and birds)	Osu	雄
Female (animals and birds)	Mesu	雌
Light aircraft	Keihikooki	軽飛行機
Sea/Marine	Umi/Kaichuu	海、海中
Island	Shima	島
Port/Harbour	Minato	港
Lake	Mizuumi	湖
Plain	Heiya	平野
Desert	Sabaku	砂漠
Mountain	Yama	山
River	Kawa	川
Gorge	Keikoku	渓谷
Rock	Iwa	岩
Sand	Suna	砂
Lookout	Miharashidai	見晴し台
Sunrise	Hinode	日の出
Sunset	Nichibotsu	日没

	ENGLISH	ROMANIZED JAPANESE	JAPANESE
480	Welcome to Australia!	Oosutoraria ni yookoso.	オーストラリアによう こそ。
481	My name is Alan. I'm pleased to meet you.	Watashi no namae wa Aran desu. Doozo yoroshiku.	私の名前はアランです。ど うぞよろしく。
482	I had a good time with all of you, too.	Watashi mo minasan to issho de tanoshikatta desu.	私も皆さんと一緒で楽しか ったです。
483	I'll see you again tomorrow.	Mata, ashita oai shimashoo.	又、あしたお会いしましょ う。
484	Please come again.	Mata, doozo irashite kudasai.	又、どうぞいらして下さい。
485	I hope to see you in Japan.	Nihon de aimashoo.	日本で会いましょう。
486	I'll take a photo for you.	Shashin o totte agemashoo.	写真を撮ってあげましょう。
487	Nice smile!	Nikkori waratte kudasai.	にっこり笑って下さい。
488	Ready? Here we go. (Lit. I'm taking it now.)	Ii desu ka? Utsushimasu.	いいですか。写します。
489	You may take photos inside the building.	Tatemono no naka de shashin o tottemo ii desu.	建物の中で写真を撮っても いいです。

	ENGLISH	ROMANIZED JAPANESE	JAPANESE
490	You are not allowed to use a flash.	Furasshu o taitewa ikemasen.	フラッシュをたいてはいけません。
491	A guide will show you the inside of the building.	Gaido ga tatemono no naka o an'nai shimasu.	ガイドが建物の中を案内します。
492	Film is not sold here.	Koko dewa firumu wa utte imasen.	ここではフィルムは売っていません。
493	This is the Art Gallery.	Kore wa bijutsukan desu.	これは美術館です。
494	On your left is the court building.	Migigawa ni saibansho ga arimasu.	右側に裁判所があります。
495	That is the statue of a famous politician.	Are wa yuumeina seijika no doozoo desu.	あれは有名な政治家の銅像です。
496	This building was built 100 years ago.	Kono tatemono wa hyakunen mae ni tateraremashita.	この建物は100年前に建てられました。
497	The inside of the building is preserved as it was before.	Naibu wa mukashi no mama ni natte imasu.	内部は昔のままになっています。

	ENGLISH	ROMANIZED JAPANESE	JAPANESE
498	This church is the oldest in this city.	Kore wa kono machi de ichiban furui kyookai desu.	これはこの町で一番古い教会です。
499	This is designated as a national treasure.	Kore wa kokuhoo ni shitei sarete imasu.	これは国宝に指定されています。
500	This is a shopping area.	Koko wa shoppingugai desu.	ここはショッピング街です。
501	This is presently the most popular sightseeing spot.	Koko ga ima ichiban ninki no aru kankoo supotto desu.	ここが今一番人気のある観光スポットです。
502	There are tours which give an aerial view.	Sora kara machi o tanoshimu tsuaa mo arimasu.	空から街を楽しむツアーもあります。
503	The flying time is 90 minutes.	Hikoo jikan wa kyuujuppun desu.	飛行時間は90分です。
504	Would you like to do some wine tasting?	Wain o otameshi ni narimasen ka?	ワインをお試しになりませんか。
505	Have you got a guide map?	An'naizu o omochi ni narimashita ka?	案内図をお持ちになりましたか。

	ENGLISH	ROMANIZED JAPANESE	JAPANESE
506	It'll be handy if you carry a coat with you.	Uwagi o motte iru to anshin desu.	上衣を持っていると安心です。
507	I'm June, your guide. Pleased to meet you.	Watashi wa an'naigakari no Juun desu. Doozo yoroshiku.	私は案内係のジューンです。どうぞよろしく。
508	It will take about 3 hours to see everything in the zoo.	Doobutsuen o zenbu mawaruto, sanjikan gurai kakarimasu.	動物園を全部まわると3時間ぐらいかかります。
509	Would you like to see Australian animals only?	Oosutoraria no doobutsu dake mimashoo ka?	オーストラリアの動物だけ見ましょうか。
510	Koalas are nocturnal animals.	Koara wa yakoosei doobutsu desu.	コアラは夜行性動物です。
511	Please do not feed.	Esa wa agenaide kudasai.	えさはあげないで下さい。
512	This one is only a baby.	Kore wa mada akanboo desu.	これはまだ赤ん坊です。
513	This is the mother.	Kore wa hahaoya desu.	これは母親です。

	ENGLISH	ROMANIZED JAPANESE	JAPANESE
514	This animal is very timid.	Kono doobutsu wa totemo okubyoo desu.	この動物はとても憶病です。
515	This is a wildlife reserve.	Koko wa yasei doobutsu hogoku desu.	ここは野生動物保護区です。
516	None (of the animals) are in cages.	Min'na hanashigai ni shite arimasu.	みんな放し飼いにしてあります。
517	This opens for public viewing at 10 and 3 o'clock.	Koko wa juuji to sanji ni kookai shite imasu.	ここは10時と3時に公開しています。
518	Would you like to hold it? (i.e. animal)	Daite mimasu ka?	抱いてみますか。
519	You may feed it.	Esa o agetemo ii desu.	えさをあげてもいいです。
520	We'll show you how this dog rounds up the sheep.	Kono inu ga hitsuji o atsumeru no o omise shimasu.	この犬が羊を集めるのをお見せします。
521	Would you like to have a go at shearing?	Hitsuji no ke o katte mimasu ka?	羊の毛を刈ってみますか。

113

	ENGLISH	ROMANIZED JAPANESE	JAPANESE
522	Would you like to have a go at milking?	Ushi no chichi o shibotte mimasu ka?	牛の乳をしぼってみますか。
523	This is the national flower.	Kore wa kokka desu.	これは国花です。
524	Would you like to go on a boat trip?	Yuuransen ni onori ni narimasu ka?	遊覧船にお乗りになりますか。
525	It's a glass-bottomed boat.	Funazoko ga garasubari no fune desu.	船底がガラス張りの船です。
526	This is the world's largest coral reef.	Sekai ichi ookii sangoshoo desu.	世界一大きいサンゴ礁です。
527	You can view the marine life from a submersible.	Suichuu kansokusen dewa umi no seibutsu ga miraremasu.	水中観測船では、海の生物が見られます。
528	You can see them at the aquarium.	Suizokukan de miraremasu.	水族館で見られます。

12 At the hotel

[1] See also 20. Illness and injuries.
21. Accidents and emergency: It's out of order,
Emergency, Theft and road accident.

At the hotel

ENGLISH	ROMANIZED JAPANESE	JAPANESE
Hotel	Hoteru	ホテル
Booking/Reservation	Yoyaku	予約
Twin room	Tsuin no heya	ツインの部屋
Double room	Daburu no heya	ダブルの部屋
Triple room	San'ninbeya	3人部屋
Room with bath	Furotsuki no heya	風呂付きの部屋
Room charge	Shukuhakuryoo	宿泊料
－ night stay	－ ppaku/－ haku	～泊
Charge	Ryookin	料金
Extra charge	Betsu ryookin	別料金
With breakfast	Chooshokutsuki	朝食付き
Vacancy	Akibeya	空き部屋
Cancellation	Torikeshi/Kyanseru	取り消し、キャンセル
Check-out time	Chekkuauto no jikan	チェックアウトの時間
Address	Juusho	住所
Name	Namae	名前
Room number	Heya bangoo	部屋番号

ENGLISH	ROMANIZED JAPANESE	JAPANESE
～ floor	～ kai	～階
Basement-floor	Chika ～ kai	地下～階
Stairs	Kaidan	階段
Porter	Pootaa	ポーター
Morning call/Wake-up call	Mooningu kooru	モーニングコール
Breakfast order form	Chooshoku no chuumonsho	朝食の注文書
Couch/Sofa	Sofaa	ソファ
Child's bed	Kodomoyoo no beddo	子供用のベッド
Bath tub	Furo/Yokusoo	**風呂、浴槽**
Wet/Flooding	Mizubitashi	水浸し
Compensation	Songaikin	損害金
Outside call	Gaisen	外線
Room service	Ruumu saabisu	ルームサービス
Emergency exit	Hijooguchi	非常口
Automatic lock	Jidoo rokku	自動ロック
Key	Kagi	鍵

ENGLISH	ROMANIZED JAPANESE	JAPANESE
Valuables	Kichoohin	貴重品
Dining room	Shokudoo	食堂
Laundry	Sentakumono	洗濯物
Does not work	Koshoochuu	故障中
Sightseeing tour	Kankoo tsuaa	観光ツァー
House doctor	Senzoku no isha	専属の医者
Doctor's visit	Ooshin	往診
Medicine	Kusuri	薬
Person in charge	Kakari no mono	係の者
Telephone operator	Denwa kookanshu	電話交換手
Page	Yobidashi	呼び出し
Message	Dengon	伝言
Deposit	Maebarai	前払い
Service charge	Saabisuryoo	サービス料
Account	Kaikei	会計
Hotel bill	Hoteru no kanjoosho	ホテルの勘定書
Mistake	Machigai	間違い

118

	ENGLISH	ROMANIZED JAPANESE	JAPANESE
529	May I have your name, please?	Dochirasama desu ka?	どちら様ですか。
530	Would you like a twin room?	Tsuin no heya ga ii desu ka?	ツインの部屋がいいですか。
531	Would you like a room with a view?	Keshiki ga mieru heya ga ii desu ka?	景色が見える部屋がいいですか。
532	It will be a triple room.	San'ninbeya ni narimasu.	3人部屋になります。
533	It's a room with bath.	Ofurotsuki no heya desu.	お風呂付きの部屋です。
534	It's a room with shower only.	Shawaa dake no heya desu.	シャワーだけの部屋です。
535	How many nights are you staying?	Nan'nichi otomari desu ka?	何日お泊りですか。
536	The room charge is $100 for one night.	Shukuhakuryoo wa ippaku hyakudoru desu.	宿泊料は1泊100ドルです。
537	The charge includes breakfast.	Ryookin wa chooshokutsuki desu.	料金は朝食付きです。

	ENGLISH	ROMANIZED JAPANESE	JAPANESE
538	Breakfast is not included in the charge.	Ryookin niwa chooshoku wa fukumarete imasen.	料金には朝食は含まれていません。
539	We have no vacancies.	Akibeya ga arimasen.	空き部屋がありません。
540	Would you like to cancel the reservation?	Yoyaku o torikeshimasu ka?	予約を取り消しますか。
541	We have to charge you a cancellation fee.	Torikeshiryoo ga kakarimasu.	取り消し料がかかります。
542	Please write your name and address.	Onamae to gojuusho o okaki kudasai.	**お名前とご住所をお書き下さい。**
543	Please sign here.	Koko ni sain o onegai shimasu.	ここにサインをお願いします。
544	You may write in Japanese.	Nihongo de kekkoo desu.	日本語で結構です。
545	Please write in English.	Eigo de onegai shimasu.	英語でお願いします。
546	This is your room number.	Kore ga heya bangoo desu.	これが部屋番号です。
547	Your room is on the 10th floor.	Heya wa jukkai desu.	部屋は10階です。

	ENGLISH	ROMANIZED JAPANESE	JAPANESE
548	The elevator is that way.	Erebeetaa wa achira desu.	エレベーターはあちらです。
549	The porter will show you the way.	Pootaa ga goan'nai shimasu.	ポーターがご案内します。
550	You may use the room until 12 o'clock.	Oheya wa juuniji made tsukaemasu.	お部屋は12時まで使えます。
551	The room is not ready yet.	Mada oheya ni hairemasen.	まだお部屋に入れません。
552	The room is ready now.	Oheya no yooi ga dekimashita.	お部屋の用意ができました。
553	Will you need a morning call?	Mooningu kooru ga irimasu ka?	モーニングコールが要りますか。
554	At what time shall I call you?	Nanji ni denwa shimashoo ka?	何時に電話しましょうか。
555	This is an order form for breakfast.	Chooshoku no chuumonsho desu.	朝食の注文書です。
556	This couch converts to a bed.	Kono sofaa ga beddo ni narimasu.	このソファがベッドになります。

	ENGLISH	ROMANIZED JAPANESE	JAPANESE
557	I'll bring a child's bed.	Kodomoyoo no beddo o motte kimasu.	子供用のベッドを持って来ます。
558	The bath takes only 3 minutes to fill.	Ofuro wa sanpun de ippai ni narimasu.	お風呂は3分でいっぱいになります。
559	Please watch that it doesn't overflow.	Afurenai yoo ni ki o tsukete kudasai.	あふれないように気をつけて下さい。
560	If you let the carpet get wet you will have to pay for the damage.	Kaapetto o mizubitashi ni suru to songaikin ga kakarimasu.	カーペットを水浸しにすると損害金がかかります。
561	Please push 9 to get an outside line.	Gaisen wa kyuuban o oshite kudasai.	外線は9番を押して下さい。
562	The emergency exit is at the end of the hall.	Hijooguchi wa rooka no tsukiatari desu.	非常口は廊下のつきあたりです。
563	The door will lock antomatically.	Jidoo rokku no doa desu.	自動ロックのドアです。
564	Please take your room key with you when you leave your room.	Kagi o motte soto ni dete kudasai.	鍵を持って外に出て下さい。

	ENGLISH	ROMANIZED JAPANESE	JAPANESE
565	Please do not leave valuables in the room.	Kichoohin wa heya ni okanaide kudasai.	貴重品は部屋に置かないで下さい。
566	Have an enjoyable stay.	Doozo, goyukkuri.	どうぞ、ごゆっくり。
567	The breakfast in the dining room is served from 7 o'clock.	Shokudoo deno chooshoku wa shichiji kara desu.	食堂での朝食は7時からです。
568	Please ask for room service.	Ruumu saabisu o tanonde kudasai.	ルームサービスを頼んで下さい。
569	Do you wish me to add this to your bill?	Ryookin wa hoteru no kanjoosho ni tsukemashoo ka?	料金はホテルの勘定書につけましょうか。
570	What is your room number?	Heya bangoo wa nanban desu ka?	部屋番号は何番ですか。
571	Please leave your laundry out by 5 p.m.	Sentakumono wa gogo goji made ni dashite kudasai.	洗濯物は午後5時までに出して下さい。
572	It will be delivered to you by 8 a.m. on the following day.	Tsugi no hi no asa hachiji made ni todokemasu.	次の日の朝8時までに届けます。

	ENGLISH	ROMANIZED JAPANESE	JAPANESE
573	You can book a tour at the information desk.	An'naijo de tsuaa no yoyaku ga dekimasu.	案内所でツアーの予約ができます。
574	I'll call the hotel house doctor for you.	Hoteru senzoku no isha o yobimashoo.	ホテル専属の医者を呼びましょう。
575	The doctor will come to see you at 7 o'clock.	Isha wa shichiji ni ooshin ni kimasu.	医者は7時に往診に来ます。
576	We'll buy the prescribed medicine and deliver it to your room.	Shohoosen no kusuri wa katte heya ni todokemasu.	処方せんの薬は買って部屋に届けます。
577	We'll have a person in charge come to your room immediately.	Sugu kakari no mono ga heya ni ukagaimasu.	すぐ係の者が部屋に伺います。
578	I'll get someone who speaks Japanese.	Nihongo o hanaseru hito o yonde kimasu.	日本語を話せる人を呼んで来ます。
579	When will you be leaving?	Itsu otachi desu ka?	いつお発ちですか。

	ENGLISH	ROMANIZED JAPANESE	JAPANESE
580	At what time shall I get someone to come for your luggage?	Nanji ni nimotsu o torini ikimashoo ka?	何時に荷物を取りに行きましょうか。
581	Did you use anything in the mini bar?	Mini baa o goriyoo ni narimashita ka?	ミニバーをご利用になりましたか。
582	I'm sorry, I made a mistake. /I was wrong.	Sumimasen. Machigaemashita.	すみません。間違えました。
583	We'll mind your luggage.	Nimotsu wa oazukari shite okimasu.	荷物はお預かりしておきます。
584	Hello. (when someone returns)	Okaerinasai.	お帰りなさい。
585	Did you enjoy the penguin tour?	Pengin tsuaa wa ikaga deshita ka?	ペンギンツアーはいかがでしたか。
586	Have a nice rest.	Yukkuri oyasumi kudasai.	ゆっくりお休み下さい。
587	There's a message for you.	Dengon ga haitte imasu.	伝言が入っています。

	ENGLISH	ROMANIZED JAPANESE	JAPANESE
588	We've put your luggage in your room.	Nimotsu o heya ni todokemashita.	荷物を部屋に届けました。
589	I'm sorry to have inconvenienced you.	Gomeiwaku o okake shimashita.	ご迷惑をおかけしました。
590	Please accept our sincere apologies.	Hontoo ni mooshiwake gozaimasen.	本当に申し訳けございません。
591	We look forward to seeing you again.	Mata, omachi shite orimasu.	又、お待ちしております。

13 At the restaurant

ENGLISH	ROMANIZED JAPANESE	JAPANESE
Restaurant	Resutoran	レストラン
Dining room	Shokudoo	食堂
Meal	Shokuji	食事
Breakfast	Chooshoku	朝食
Lunch	Ranchi/Chuushoku	ランチ、昼食
Snacks	Keishoku	軽食
Set (table d'hôte) menu	Teishoku	定食
à la carte	Ippin ryoori	一品料理
Take away/Fast food	Teekuauto	テークアウト
Japanese cuisine	Nihon ryoori	日本料理
Italian cuisine	Itaria ryoori	イタリア料理
French cuisine	Furansu ryoori	フランス料理
Chinese cuisine	Chuuka ryoori	中華料理
Buffet/Smorgasbord	Baikingu sutairu	バイキングスタイル
Chef's recommendation	Osusumehin	おすすめ品
Hors d'oeuvres/Appetizers	Oodoburu/Zensai	オードブル、前菜

ENGLISH	ROMANIZED JAPANESE	JAPANESE
Dessert	Dezaato	デザート
Black tea	Koocha	紅茶
Tasty/Delicious	Oishii	おいしい
Hot (e.g. soup)	Atsui	あつい
Cold	Tsumetai	つめたい
Sweet	Amai	あまい
Hot (e.g. chili)	Karai	辛い
Fresh	Shinsenna	新鮮な
Seafood	Shiifuudo	シーフード
Fish	Sakana	魚
The local product	Tochi no meisan	土地の名産
Meat dish	Nikuryoori	肉料理
Beef	Biifu/Gyuuniku	ビーフ、牛肉
Medium rare	midiamu reaa	ミディアムレアー
Pork	Pooku/Butaniku	ポーク、豚肉
Chicken	Chikin/Toriniku	チキン、鳥肉

ENGLISH	ROMANIZED JAPANESE	JAPANESE
Egg	Tamago	卵
Vegetable	Yasai	野菜
Bread	Pan	パン
Rice	Raisu/Gohan	ライス，ご飯
Salt	Shio	塩
Pepper	Koshoo	こしょう
Sugar	Satoo	砂糖
Spices	Kooshinryoo	香辛料
Drinks	Nomimono	飲み物
Beer	Biiru	ビール
Water	Mizu	水
Serving trolley	Ryooriyoo wagon	料理用ワゴン
Reservations	Yoyaku	予約
Order	Chuumon	注文
Closed	Heiten	閉店
Tax	Zeikin	税金
Bill	Kanjoosho	勘定書

	ENGLISH	ROMANIZED JAPANESE	JAPANESE
592	Would you like to book?	Goyoyaku desu ka?	ご予約ですか。
593	3 persons at 7.30 today. Is that correct?	Kyoo no shichijihan ni sanmeisama desu ne.	今日の7時半に3名様ですね。
594	Thank you very much./ Certainly./With pleasure.	Kashikomarimashita.	かしこまりました。
595	We'll see you then./We'll look forward to seeing you (then).	Omachishite orimasu.	お待ちしております。
596	I'm sorry, but we are fully booked.	Ainiku kono jikan wa man'in desu.	あいにく、この時間は満員です。
597	You can book for 6 o'clock. How would that be?	Rokuji nara aite imasu ga.	6時ならあいていますが。
598	I see. I'm sorry.	Soo desu ka? Sumimasen.	そうですか。すみません。
599	Breakfast is served from 7 until 9 o'clock.	Chooshoku wa shichiji kara kuji made desu.	朝食は7時から9時までです。
600	We are open for dinner from 6 o'clock.	Yuushoku wa rokuji kara desu.	夕食は6時からです。

	ENGLISH	ROMANIZED JAPANESE	JAPANESE
601	We are closed from 4 to 6 o'clock.	Yoji kara rokuji made shimarimasu.	4時から6時まで閉まります。
602	We do not open on Sundays.	Nichiyoobi wa kyuugyoo desu.	日曜日は休業です。
603	You need to wear a tie and jacket in the restaurant.	Resutoran dewa, nekutai to uwagi o kinakereba narimasen.	レストランでは、ネクタイと上衣を着なければなりません。
604	Hello! (welcoming to the restaurant)	Irasshaimase.	いらっしゃいませ。
605	May I have your name?	Dochirasama desu ka?	どちら様ですか。
606	You have a reservation for 4 (persons)?	Yonmeisama desu ne.	4名様ですね。
607	Under whose name is your party booked?	Donata no namae de yoyaku sarete imasu ka?	どなたの名前で予約されていますか。
608	Would you mind waiting here for a moment?	Kochira de shooshoo omachi kudasai.	こちらで少々お待ち下さい。

	ENGLISH	ROMANIZED JAPANESE	JAPANESE
609	I'm sorry to have kept you waiting. Please come this way.	Omataseshimashita. Doozo, kochirae.	お待たせしました。どうぞ こちらへ。
610	Would you like some drinks?	Onomimono wa ikaga desu ka?	お飲み物はいかがですか。
611	Which kind of juice would you like?	Juusu wa nani ga ii desu ka?	ジュースは何がいいですか。
612	Would you like your whisky straight, or with water?	Uisukii wa sutoreeto desu ka mizuwari desu ka?	ウイスキーは、ストレート ですか、水割りですか。
613	Would you like red or white wine?	Wain wa aka desu ka, shiro desu ka?	ワインは赤ですか、白です か。
614	This is an Australian wine.	Kore wa Oosutoraria san no wain desu.	これはオーストラリア産の ワインです。
615	This wine is very dry.	Kono wain wa karakuchi desu.	このワインは辛口です。
616	Would you prefer a less dry wine?	Amari karakuchi de nai hoo ga ii desu ka?	あまり辛口でない方がいい ですか。

	ENGLISH	ROMANIZED JAPANESE	JAPANESE
617	This will suit a meat dish.	Kore wa nikuryoori ni aimasu.	これは肉料理に合います。
618	You can order wine by the glass.	Wain wa gurasu demo chuumon dekimasu.	ワインはグラスでも注文できます。
619	We do not serve alcohol.	Osakerui wa oite arimasen.	お酒類は置いてありません。
620	You may bring your own alcohol.	Osakerui wa gojisan kudasai.	お酒類はご持参下さい。
621	The menu is on the wall there.	Menyuu wa achira no kabe ni gozaimasu.	メニューはあちらの壁にございます。
622	May I take your order now?	Gochuumon wa nani ni nasaimasu ka?	ご注文は何になさいますか。
623	This is today's chef's recommendation.	Kore wa kyoo no osusume ryoori desu.	これは今日のおすすめ料理です。
624	This is a speciality of this restaurant.	Kore wa tooten no tokubetsu ryoori desu.	これは当店の特別料理です。
625	It's fresh fish caught today.	Kyoo toreta shinsen na sakana desu.	今日獲れた新鮮な魚です。

	ENGLISH	ROMANIZED JAPANESE	JAPANESE
626	I'm sorry, we don't have this today.	Ainiku kore wa ima kirashite orimasu.	あいにくこれは今、きらしております。
627	The oysters are a local product.	Kaki wa kono tochi no meisan desu.	かきは、この土地の名産です。
628	We can prepare a platter of assorted seafood.	Shiifuudo no moriawase mo dekimasu.	シーフードの盛り合わせもできます。
629	The set menu includes bread and salad.	Teishoku niwa pan to sarada ga tsukimasu.	定食にはパンとサラダがつきます。
630	Would you like to have salad first?	Sarada wa saisho ni meshiagarimasu ka?	サラダは最初に召し上がりますか。
631	Shall I bring it with the main course?	Mein koosu to issho ni omochi shimashoo ka?	メインコースと一緒にお持ちしましょうか。
632	How would you like your steak cooked?	Suteeki no yakiguai wa dooshimashoo ka?	ステーキの焼き具合は、どうしましょうか。
633	This dish is served with sauce over it.	Kono ryoori wa ue ni soosu ga kakatte imasu.	この料理は上にソースがかかっています。
634	The sauce is served in a separate dish.	Soosu wa betsu ni kimasu.	ソースは別に来ます。

	ENGLISH	ROMANIZED JAPANESE	JAPANESE
635	This is home-made ice cream.	Jikasei no aisukuriimu desu.	自家製のアイスクリームです。
636	Which would you like, tea or coffee?	Koohii to koocha to dochira ga ii desu ka?	コーヒーと紅茶とどちらがいいですか。
637	When your number is called, please come to get it.	Bangoo o yondara, torini kite kudasai.	番号を呼んだら、取りに来て下さい。
638	Please pay now.	Saki ni okane o haratte kudasai.	先にお金を払って下さい。
639	Please tell me what you like.	Osukina mono o itte kudasai.	お好きなものを言って下さい。
640	Please help yourself to whatever you like.	Osukinamono o gojiyuu ni osara ni otori kudasai.	お好きなものをご自由にお皿におとり下さい。
641	Instead of putting everything on the plate at once, come back as often as you like.	Ichido ni zenbu osara ni nosezu ni, nando kitemo ii desu.	1度に全部お皿にのせずに、何度来てもいいです。
642	Please start with the soup.	Suupu kara doozo.	スープからどうぞ。

	ENGLISH	ROMANIZED JAPANESE	JAPANESE
643	We will bring tea and coffee to your table.	Koohii to koocha wa teeburu ni omochi shimasu.	コーヒーと紅茶はテーブルにお持ちします。
644	Would you like anything else? This will be the last order.	Rasuto oodaa ni narimasu ga, tsuika chuumon wa gozaimasen ka?	ラストオーダーになりますが、追加注文はございませんか。
645	Did I give you the wrong order?	Gochuumon no shina to chigaimashita ka?	ご注文の品と違いましたか。
646	I am very sorry.	Taihen shitsurei shimashita.	たいへん失礼しました。
647	I'm sorry, would you say the orders again, please?	Sumimasen. Moo ichido chuumon o osshatte kudasai.	すみません。もう一度注文をおっしゃって下さい。
648	We will change it straight away.	Suguni otorikae shimasu.	すぐにおとりかえします。
649	I'm sorry, we cannot take any more orders.	Sumimasen. Moo chuumon wa owarimashita.	すみません。もう注文は終わりました。
650	Would you like to pay separately?	Okaikei wa betsubetsu desu ka?	お会計は別々ですか。

	ENGLISH	ROMANIZED JAPANESE	JAPANESE
651	It's $50 per person.	Ohitorisama gojuudoru desu.	お１人様50ドルです。
652	We accept credit cards.	Kurejitto kaado demo kekkoo desu.	クレジットカードでも結構です。
653	Excuse me. Here's your change.	Moshimoshi, otsuri desu.	もしもし、おつりです。
654	Thank you very much. Please come again.	Arigatoo gozaimashita. Mata, doozo.	ありがとうございました。又、どうぞ。

Shopping

[1] See also 21. Accidents and emergency: Refund and exchange.

ENGLISH	ROMANIZED JAPANESE	JAPANESE
Shopping	Kaimono/Shoppingu	買物、ショッピング
Shop/Store	Mise/Shooten	店、商店
Shopping area	Shootengai	商店街
Department store	Depaato	デパート
Card (financial)	Kaado	カード
Speciality store	Senmonten	専門店
Duty-free shop	Menzeihinten	免税品店
Souvenir shop	Miyagemonoten	みやげもの店
Folk handicrafts shop	Mingeihinten	民芸品店
Boutique	Butikku	ブティック
High-quality dress shop	Kookyuu yoohinten	高級洋品店
Shoe shop	Kutsuya	靴屋
Brand product	Burando seihin	ブランド製品
Leather goods	Kawa seihin	皮製品
Imported goods	Yunyuuhin	輸入品
Australian-made	Oosutorariasei	オーストラリア製
Pure wool	Junmoo	純毛

ENGLISH	ROMANIZED JAPANESE	JAPANESE
Sports goods	Supootsu yoohin	スポーツ用品
Gentlemen's wear	Shinshi yoohin	神士用品
Ladies' wear	Fujin yoohin	婦人用品
Childrens' wear	Kodomo yoohin	子供用品
Toys	Omocha	おもちゃ
Golf supplies	Gorufu yoohin	ゴルフ用品
― floor	― Kai	～階
Foodstuff	Shokuryoohin	食料品
Local product	Genchi tokusanhin	現地特産品
Genuine	Honmono	本物
Handmade	Tezukuri	手作り
Gift	Okurimono	贈物
Souvenir	Omiyage	おみやげ
Cosmetics	Keshoohin	化粧品
Jewellery	Hooseki	宝石
Price	Nedan	値段
Fixed price	Teika	定価

ENGLISH	ROMANIZED JAPANESE	JAPANESE
Special price	Tokka	特価
Half-price	Hangaku	半額
20% discount	Nijuppaasento biki	20パーセント引き
Bargain	**Baagen**	バーゲン
Expensive	Takai	高い
Cheap	Yasui	安い
Change	Otsuri	おつり
Total (amount)	Gookei	合計
Out of stock	Shinagire	品切れ
Gift wrapping	Zootooyoo hoosoo	贈答用包装
Exchange	Torikae	とりかえ
Posting	Yuusoo	郵送
Postage	Yuusooryoo	郵送料
Insurance	Hoken	保険
Recipient's name	Uketorinin no namae	受取人の名前
Address	Juusho	住所

	ENGLISH	ROMANIZED JAPANESE	JAPANESE
655	Hello. May I help you?	Irasshaimase.	いらっしゃいませ。
656	We have duty-free goods in the basement.	Menzeihin wa chika ni gozaimasu.	免税品は地下にございます。
657	The souvenirs are on the first (ground) floor.	Miyagemono wa ikkai desu.	みやげ物は1階です。
658	We can offer 10 per cent off any souvenirs.	Miyagemono wa dore mo ichiwari ohiki shimasu.	みやげ物はどれも1割お引きします。
659	We have Japanese-speaking staff.	Nihongo ga wakaru ten'in ga orimasu.	日本語がわかる店員がおります。
660	We are open from 9 until 6 o'clock.	Kono mise wa kuji kara rokuji made desu.	この店は9時から6時までです。
661	We are open for business on the weekends, too.	Do, nichi mo eigyoo shite orimasu.	土、日も営業しております。
662	We are not open on Sundays.	Nichiyoobi wa kyuugyoo desu.	日曜日は休業です。
663	About how much do you intend to spend?	Goyosan wa donokurai desu ka?	ご予算はどの位ですか。

	ENGLISH	ROMANIZED JAPANESE	JAPANESE
664	This is a special product of this country.	Kore wa kono kuni no tokusanhin desu.	これはこの国の特産品です。
665	This is Italian-made.	Kore wa Itariyasei desu.	これはイタリヤ製です。
666	This is an example of folk handicraft unique to this country.	Kore wa kono kuni tokusan no shukoogeihin desu.	これはこの国特産の手工芸品です。
667	This is genuine leather.	Kore wa honmono no kawa desu.	これは本物の皮です。
668	Which brand are you after?	Dono burando o osagashi desu ka?	どのブランドをおさがしですか。
669	Sorry, we do not carry that brand.	Sumimasen, sono burando wa atsukatte orimasen.	すみません、そのブランドは扱っておりません。
670	Sorry, that is out of stock at present.	Ainiku shinagire ni natte imasu.	あいにく品切れになっています。
671	You can pay by cash, card or travellers cheque.	Oshiharai wa genkin demo, kaado demo, toraberaazu chekku demo kekkoo desu.	お支払いは現金でも、カードでも、トラベラーズチェックでも結構です。

	ENGLISH	ROMANIZED JAPANESE	JAPANESE
672	I'll show it to you now.	Ima omise shimasu.	今お見せします。
673	Wait a moment, please.	Chotto omachi kudasai.	ちょっとお待ち下さい。
674	What is the size?	Saizu wa ikutsu desu ka?	サイズはいくつですか。
675	We have a smaller size as well.	Motto chiisai saizu mo arimasu.	もっと小さいサイズもあります。
676	How old is the child?	Okosan wa oikutsu desu ka?	お子さんはおいくつですか。
677	I'll take your measurements.	Saizu o hakarimashoo.	サイズを計りましょう。
678	Would you like to try it on?	Shichaku nasai masu ka?	試着なさいますか。
679	That looks very nice on you.	Totemo yoku oniai desu.	とてもよくお似合いです。
680	This has just been reduced (in price).	Kore wa ima yasuku natte imasu.	これは今安くなっています。
681	Japanese people like this very much.	**Kore wa Nihon no kata ni totemo yorokobarete imasu.**	これは日本の方にとてもよろこばれています。
682	Is this for a gift?	Okurimono desu ka?	贈物ですか。

	ENGLISH	ROMANIZED JAPANESE	JAPANESE
683	I'll gift wrap it for you.	Okurimonoyoo ni hoosoo shimashoo.	贈物用に包装しましょう。
684	Do you want me to remove the price tag?	Shoofuda o torimashoo ka?	正札をとりましょうか。
685	Do you want us to keep this until tomorrow?	Asu made totte okimashoo ka?	明日までとっておきましょうか。
686	We'll deliver this to your hotel by the evening.	Yuugata made ni hoteru ni todokemasu.	夕方までにホテルに届けます。
687	Would you tell me your room number, please?	Hoteru no heya bangoo o oshiete kudasai.	ホテルの部屋番号を教えて下さい。
688	We are happy to exchange.	Otorikae dekimasu.	おとりかえ出来ます。
689	You cannot return this article.	Kono shinamono wa henpin dekimasen.	この品物は返品出来ません。
690	That's $200 altogether.	Gookei nihyakudoru desu.	合計200ドルです。
691	It'll be $180 with the 10 per cent discount.	Juppaasento hikimasu to, hyaku hachijuudoru ni narimasu.	10パーセント引きますと、180ドルになります。

	ENGLISH	ROMANIZED JAPANESE	JAPANESE
692	Please check it.	Doozo otashikame kudasai.	どうぞお確かめ下さい。
693	I'm sorry, but we can't give any more discount than that.	Kore ijoo ohiki dekinai nodesu ga.	これ以上お引き出来ないのですが。
694	We can pack and post it to Japan for you.	Kochira de hoosoo shite Nihon ni yuusoo itashimasu.	こちらで包装して日本に郵送いたします。
695	Would you like to send it by seamail or airmail?	Funabin ni shimasu ka, kookuubin ni shimasu ka?	船便にしますか、航空便にしますか。
696	The postage is $15.	Yuusooryoo wa juugodoru desu.	郵送料は15ドルです。
697	It will take about 25 days to get there.	Nijuugonichi gurai de tsukimasu.	25日位で着きます。
698	This is a warranty of purchase form.	Kore wa hoshoosho desu.	これは保証書です。
699	Please write the name and address of the recipient.	Uketorinin no juusho shimei o kaite kudasai.	受取人の住所氏名を書いて下さい。

	ENGLISH	ROMANIZED JAPANESE	JAPANESE
700	Please do not put this in a suitcase but carry it by hand.	Suutsukeesu ni irenaide, te ni motte kudasai.	スーツケースに入れないで手に持って下さい。
701	You must not open this before the customs inspection is completed.	Tsuukan suru made aketewa ikemasen.	通関するまで開けてはいけません。
702	If you open the bag, you'll be charged a fine.	Akeruto bakkin ga kakarimasu.	開けると罰金がかかります。
703	Please give this receipt to the customs officer.	Kono uketorisho o zeikan ni watashite kudasai.	この受取書を税関に渡して下さい。

15 Telephone and post office

ENGLISH	ROMANIZED JAPANESE	JAPANESE
Telephone	Denwa	電話
Public telephone/Pay phone	Kooshuu denwa	公衆電話
Telephone number	Denwa bangoo	電話番号
Telephone directory	Denwachoo	電話帳
Local calls	Shinai tsuuwa	市内通話
Telephone card	Terehon kaado	テレホン　カード
Time limit	Jikan no seigen	時間の制限
Direct call	Chokutsuu	直通
Long-distance call	Chookyori denwa	長距離電話
International call	Kokusai denwa	国際電話
Country code	Kuni bangoo	国番号
Area code	Shigai kyokuban	市外局番
Outside line	Gaisen	外線
Mobile telephone	Keitai denwa	携帯電話
Operator	Kookanshu	交換手
Collect call/Reverse charge call	Korekuto kooru	コレクトコール

ENGLISH	ROMANIZED JAPANESE	JAPANESE
Person-to-person call	Shimei tsuuwa	指名通話
Receiver	Juwaki	受話器
Call charge	Tsuuwa ryookin	通話料金
Engaged	Hanashichuu	話し中
Crossed line	Konsen	混線
Guest room	Kyakushitsu	客室
E-mail	Ii-meeru	イーメール、電子メール
Post office	Yuubinkyoku	郵便局
General Post Office	Chuuoo yuubinkyoku	中央郵便局
Mailbox	Posuto	ポスト
Letter	Tegami	手紙
Stamp	Kitte	切手
Commemorative stamp	Kinen kitte	記念切手
Postcard (picture)	Ehagaki	絵ハガキ
Aerogramme	Kookuushokan	航空書簡
Envelope	Fuutoo	封筒
How many? (e.g. stamps)	Nanmai	何枚

ENGLISH	ROMANIZED JAPANESE	JAPANESE
Airmail	Kookuubin	航空便
Seamail	Funabin	船便
Express mail/Priority paid	Sokutatsu	速達
Registered mail	Kakitome	書留
Parcel	Kozutsumi	小包
Small parcel	Kogata hoosoobutsu	小型包装物
Printed matter	Insatsubutsu	印刷物
Contents	Nakami	中味
Gift	Okurimono	贈物
Customs declaration form	Zeikan shinkokusho	税関申告書
Postage	Yuubin ryookin	郵便料金
Sender	Sashidashinin	差出人
Postal address	Atesaki	宛先
Form	Yooshi	用紙
Address/Domicile	Juusho	住所
Facsimile	Fakkusu	ファックス
Receipt	Ryooshuusho/Uketorishoo	領収書、受取証

	ENGLISH	ROMANIZED JAPANESE	JAPANESE
704	A local telephone call is 50 cents.	Shinai wa ittsuuwa gojussento desu.	市内は一通話50セントです。
705	There is no time limit.	Jikan no seigen wa arimasen.	時間の制限はありません。
706	Insert more coins when you hear the time-limit tone.	Jikan seigen no aizu ga attara okane o irete kudasai.	時間制限の合図があったらお金を入れて下さい。
707	Insert some money, and any unused coins will be returned later.	Saisho ni koin o irete okeba tsukawanakatta bun wa modorimasu.	最初にコインを入れておけば使わなかった分は戻ります。
708	You had better have a lot of coins ready.	Kooka o takusan yooishita hooga ii desu.	硬貨をたくさん用意した方がいいです。
709	You can make an international call from an ISD-marked public phone.	Ai-esu-dii maaku no kooshuu denwa kara kokusai denwa ga kakeraremasu.	ISDマークの公衆電話から国際電話がかけられます。
710	First, push the international call number, 0011.	Saisho ni kokusai denwa bangoo no zerozero ichiichi o oshite kudasai.	最初に国際電話番号の0011を押して下さい。

	ENGLISH	ROMANIZED JAPANESE	JAPANESE
711	Next, push the area code for Japan, 81.	Tsugi ni Nihon no kuni bangoo no hachiichi o oshimasu.	次に日本の国番号の81を押します。
712	Then, push the area code in Japan, excluding the first 0.	Soshite shigai kyokuban no zero o habuita bangoo o oshimasu.	そして市外局番の０をはぶいた番号を押します。
713	For instance, for calling Tokyo, you dial 0011-81-3.	Tatoeba Tookyoo nara, zerozeroichiichi-hachiichi-san desu.	例えば東京なら0011-81-3です。
714	Lastly, push the telephone number of the person.	Saigo ni aite no denwa bangoo o oshite kudasai.	最後に相手の電話番号を押して下さい。
715	You can make a direct international call from your hotel room.	Hoteru no heya kara mo kokusai denwa ga chokutsuu de kakarimasu.	ホテルの部屋からも国際電話が直通でかかります。
716	Push 0 for the outside line first.	Mazu gaisen no zero o oshite kudasai.	まず外線の０を押して下さい。
717	Please do not use mobile telephone.	Keitai denwa wa tsukawanaide kudasai.	携帯電話は使わないで下さい。

154

| --- | --- | --- | --- |
718	Push 9 for the switchboard.	Kookandai wa kyuuban desu.	交換台は9番です。
719	You can make a direct long-distance call after pushing the outside line number.	Gaisen o oshite kara chokutsuu de chookyori denwa mo kakeraremasu.	外線を押してから直通で長距離電話もかけられます。
720	To call a guestroom, just push the room number.	Kyakushitsu ni denwa suru niwa aite no heya bangoo o oshimasu.	客室に電話するには、相手の部屋番号を押します。
721	Please book reverse charge calls with the operator.	Korekutokooru wa kookanshu ni mooshikonde kudasai.	コレクトコールは交換手に申し込んで下さい。
722	Have you checked in the telephone directory?	Denwachoo de shirabemashita ka?	電話帳で調べましたか。
723	Please give me the name of the area in Japan.	Nihon no chiikimei o itte kudasai.	日本の地域名を言って下さい。
724	Would you spell it, please?	Tsuzuri o itte kudasai.	つづりを言って下さい。
725	Give me the number you want to call, please.	Aite no denwabangoo o itte kudasai.	相手の電話番号を言って下さい。

	ENGLISH	ROMANIZED JAPANESE	JAPANESE
726	Do you want a person-to-person call?	Shimeitsuuwa desu ka?	指名通話ですか。
727	What is your number?	Anata no bangoo wa nanban desu ka?	あなたの番号は何番ですか。
728	Please hold the line.	Sonomama kirazu ni omachi kudasai.	そのまま切らずにお待ち下さい。
729	I'm connecting you now.	Ima otsunagi shimasu.	今、おつなぎします。
730	Please go ahead.	Doozo ohanashi kudasai.	どうぞお話し下さい。
731	The line is engaged.	Ohanashichuu desu.	お話中です。
732	Would you like to wait?	Omachi ni narimasu ka?	お待ちになりますか。
733	The call you have just made cost $10.	Tadaimano tsuuwa wa juudoru desu.	只今の通話は10ドルです。
734	Hello. (on telephone) This is Hotel Australia.	Moshimoshi, Hoteru Oosutoraria desu.	もしもし、ホテルオーストラリアです。
735	Whom would you like to speak to?	Donata o oyobi desu ka?	どなたをお呼びですか。

	ENGLISH	ROMANIZED JAPANESE	JAPANESE
736	Hold on a moment, please.	Shooshoo omachi kudasai.	少々お待ち下さい。
737	He/She is not answering.	Okyakusama wa ode ni narimasen.	お客様はお出になりません。
738	Would you mind calling him/her again (later)?	Mata kakenaoshite kudasaimasu ka?	又、かけ直して下さいますか。
739	The post office is open from 9 to 5.	Yuubinkyoku wa kuji kara goji made desu.	郵便局は9時から5時までです。
740	They are closed on weekends and public holidays.	Shuumatsu to shukujitsu wa yasumi desu.	週末と祝日は休みです。
741	Please go to counter No. 5.	Kore wa goban no madoguchi ni itte kudasai.	これは5番の窓口に行って下さい。
742	We don't handle that at this post office.	Kore wa kono yuubinkyoku dewa atsukatte imasen.	これはこの郵便局では扱っていません。
743	You have to go to the General Post Office.	Chuuoo yuubinkyoku e itte kudasai.	中央郵便局へ行って下さい。
744	Would you like to send it by airmail or by economy?	Kookuubin desu ka, sarubin desu ka?	航空便ですか、サル便(SAL)ですか。

	ENGLISH	ROMANIZED JAPANESE·	JAPANESE
745	A postcard to Japan costs 90 cents.	Ehagaki wa Nihon made kyuujussento desu.	絵はがきは日本まで90セントです。
746	Please put airmail stickers on.	Eameeru no shiiru o hatte kudasai.	エアメールのシールをはって下さい。
747	It will take about 3 days even by express/priority paid mail.	Sokutatsu demo mikka gurai kakarimasu.	速達でも3日位かかります。
748	We have a set of commemorative stamps for sale.	Kinen kitte no setto ga arimasu.	記念切手のセットがあります。
749	What are the contents?	Nakami wa nan desu ka?	中味は何ですか。
750	We sell boxes/bags suitable for parcels.	Kozutsumi yoo no hako/ fukuro ga arimasu.	小包用の箱／袋があります。
751	There is a cheaper price for card-only mail.	Kaadò dake wa waribiki ryookin desu.	カードだけは割引料金です。
752	You must post it without sealing the envelope.	Kaifuu de dasanakereba narimasen.	開封で出さなければなりません。

16 Farmstay and homestay

[1] See also 12. At the hotel: Reservations.
[2] See also 9. Train and coach trips – Part 2: Comfort of passengers.
[3] See also 13. At the restaurant: Beverages, Selecting from the menu, Finding out customer preferences.

ENGLISH	ROMANIZED JAPANESE	JAPANESE
Homestay	Hoomusutei	ホームステイ
Farmstay	Faamusutei	ファームステイ
Near the sea	Umi no chikaku	海の近く
Near the mountains	Yama no hoo	山の方
Farm	Noojoo	農場
Homestead	Nooka	農家
Family	Kazoku	家族
(My) husband	Shujin	主人
(My) wife	Tsuma	妻
Son	Musuko	息子
Daughter	Musume	娘
― years old	― sai	～才
Friend	Tomodachi	友達
Neighbour	Kinjo no hito	近所の人
4 nights stay	Yonpaku	4泊
With meals	Shokujitsuki	食事付
3 meals	Sanshoku	3食

ENGLISH	ROMANIZED JAPANESE	JAPANESE
Breakfast	Chooshoku	朝食
Lunch	**Ranchi/Chuushoku**	**ランチ、昼食**
Dinner	Yuushoku	夕食
Cook for yourself	Jisui	自炊
Map	Chizu	地図
Station	Eki	駅
Person to meet you	Mukae no hito	迎えの人
Room	Heya	部屋
Living room/Sitting room	Ima	居間
Dining room	Shokudoo	食堂
Kitchen	Daidokoro	台所
Bath	Furo	風呂
Hot water	Oyu	お湯
Fan	Senpuuki	扇風機
Adjusting a heater	Hiitaa no choosetsu	ヒーターの調節
Hot	Atsui	あつい
Cold	Samui	寒い

ENGLISH	ROMANIZED JAPANESE	JAPANESE
Desk lamp	Denki sutando	電気スタンド
Plug (electricity)	Sashikomi	さし込み
Key	Kagi	鍵
Coat-hanger	Hangaa	ハンガー
Blanket	Moofu	毛布
Refrigerator	Reizooko	冷蔵庫
At what time?	Nanji ni	何時に
Meat	Niku	肉
Cow	Ushi	牛
Beef	Gyuuniku	牛肉
Calf	Koushi	子牛
Veal	Koushi no niku	子牛の肉
Sheep	Hitsuji	羊
Lamb	Kohitsuji	子羊
Horse	Uma	馬
Horse riding	Jooba	乗馬

	ENGLISH	ROMANIZED JAPANESE	JAPANESE
753	This is a farm near the sea.	Koko wa umi no chikaku no noojoo desu.	ここは海の近くの農場です。
754	It's $60 a day with 3 meals.	Sanshokutsuki de ippaku rokujuudoru desu.	3食付で1泊60ドルです。
755	I have booked for 5 days from Monday.	Getsuyoobi kara itsukakan yoyaku shimashita.	月曜日から5日間予約しました。
756	It's here on this map.	Kono chizu de koko desu.	この地図でここです。
757	Someone will come to the station to meet you.	Eki ni mukae no hito ga kite imasu.	駅に迎えの人が来ています。
758	It is a family by the name of Collins.	Korinzu-san to yuu kazoku desu.	コリンズさんという家族です。
759	Hello. You are Ms Tanaka?	Kon'nichiwa, Tanaka-san desu ne.	こんにちは、田中さんですね。
760	I am Tom Collins. Nice to meet you.	Watashi wa Tomu Korinzu desu. Hajimemashite.	私はトム コリンズです。はじめまして。
761	Please call me Tom.	Doozo Tomu to yonde kudasai.	どうぞトムと呼んで下さい。

	ENGLISH	ROMANIZED JAPANESE	JAPANESE
762	Meet my family. This is my wife, Lyn.	Watashi no kazoku desu. Tsuma no Rin desu.	私の家族です。妻のリンです。
763	My son, Peter. He is 10 years old.	Musuko no Piitaa desu. Jussai desu.	息子のピーターです。10才です。
764	This is my daughter, Cathy. She is 6.	Musume no Kyashii desu. Rokusai desu.	娘のキャシーです。6才です。
765	My eldest son is at boarding school in the city.	Choonan wa tokai no gakkoo no ryoo ni imasu.	長男は都会の学校の寮にいます。
766	Please consider yourself one of the family, and make yourself at home.	Doozo kazoku no yooni kiraku ni osugoshi kudasai.	どうぞ家族のように気楽にお過ごし下さい。
767	This is the living room and that is the dining room.	Koko ga ima de achira ga shokudoo desu.	ここが居間であちらが食堂です。
768	Your room is upstairs.	Anata no heya wa nikai desu.	あなたの部屋は2階です。
769	There are extra blankets here.	**Moofu wa koko nimo arimasu.**	**毛布はここにもあります。**

770	To turn the heater up, do this.	Hiitaa wa koosuruto atsuku narimasu.	ヒーターはこうするとあつくなります。
771	The tap on the left is for hot water.	Hidari no jaguchi ga oyu desu.	左の蛇口がお湯です。
772	You can have a bath whenever you like.	Osukina toki ni ofuro ni haitte kudasai.	お好きな時にお風呂に入って下さい。
773	Do you want to use a hair dryer?	Heyaa doraiyaa o tsukaitai desu ka?	ヘヤードライヤーを使いたいですか。
774	Will you need a heater?	Hiitaa wa irimasu ka?	ヒーターは要りますか。
775	Please feel free to ask for whatever you need.	Nani ka hitsuyoona mono ga attara osshatte kudasai.	何か必要なものがあったらおっしゃって下さい。
776	Please eat and drink anything you like from the refrigerator.	Reizooko no naka no mono mo jiyuu ni tsukatte kudasai.	冷蔵庫の中の物も自由に使って下さい。
777	At about what time would you like to go to bed?	Nanji goro yasumimasu ka?	何時頃休みますか。
778	At what time do you get up?	Nanji ni okimasu ka?	何時に起きますか。

	ENGLISH	ROMANIZED JAPANESE	JAPANESE
779	At what time would you like to have breakfast?	Chooshoku wa nanji ga ii desu ka?	朝食は何時がいいですか。
780	At what time are you going out?	Nanji ni dekakemasu ka?	何時に出かけますか。
781	The meal is ready.	Shokuji no yooi ga dekimashita.	食事の用意が出来ました。
782	Do you like meat?	Niku wa osuki desu ka?	肉はお好きですか。
783	This is a cake I made myself.	Watashi ga tsukutta keeki desu.	私が作ったケーキです。
784	This is very tasty.	Totemo oishii desu yo.	とてもおいしいですよ。
785	Would you like to have some more?	Moosukoshi ikaga desu ka?	もう少しいかがですか。
786	We have enjoyed having you.	Watashitachi mo tanoshikatta desu.	私達も楽しかったです。
787	Take care. Please come again.	Doozo ki o tsukete. Mata doozo.	どうぞ気をつけて。又どうぞ。

17 Sports

[1] See also 13. At the restaurant: Taking a booking.
[2] See also 19. Climate and clothing: Today's weather, Tomorrow's weather will be…, Bad weather.

ENGLISH	ROMANIZED JAPANESE	JAPANESE
Sport	Supootsu	スポーツ
Olympic Games	Orinpikku taikai	オリンピック大会
Stadium	Kyoogijoo/Sutajiamu	競技場、スタジアム
Sports (ground, oval)/Arena	Gurando	グランド
Practice ground/Centre	Renshuujoo	練習場
Team	Chiimu	チーム
Match/Competition	Shiai	試合
Night match	Yakanjiai	夜間試合
Race	Reesu	レース
Indoor sports	Shitsunai supootsu	室内スポーツ
Outdoor sports	Okugai supootsu	屋外スポーツ
Sports supplies	Supootsu yoohin	スポーツ用品
Instructor	Insutorakutaa	インストラクター
Lecture/Instruction	Kooshuu	講習
Beginner	Shoshinsha	初心者
Registration	Tooroku	登録
Licence	Raisensu	ライセンス

ENGLISH	ROMANIZED JAPANESE	JAPANESE
Safe	Anzen	安全
Danger	Kiken	危険
Dangerous	Abunai	あぶない
Weather	Tenki/Tenkoo	天気、天候
Bad conditions	Kondishon ga warui	コンディションが悪い
Membership	Kaiinsei	会員制
Weekend	Shuumatsu	週末
Weekdays	Heijitsu	平日
(Golf) clubs for hire	Kashi kurabu	貸クラブ
Right-handed	Migikiki	右利き
Left-handed	Hidarikiki	左利き
Deposit	Depojitto	デポジット
Swimming	Suiei	水泳
Swimming in the sea	Kaisuiyoku	海水浴
Area where swimming is permitted	Yuuei kuiki	遊泳区域
Water skiing	Suijoo sukii	水上スキー

ENGLISH	ROMANIZED JAPANESE	JAPANESE
Ski resort	Sukiijoo	スキー場
Bicycle	Jitensha	自転車
Mountain climbing	Tozan	登山
Horse riding	Jooba	乗馬
Horse-racing/Races	Keiba/Hoosu reesu	競馬、ホースレース
Sea/Beach	Umi	海
River/Stream	Kawa	川
Lake	Mizuumi	湖
Fishing	Tsuri	釣り
Fishing gear	Tsuri doogu	釣り道具
Boat	Fune/Booto	船、ボート
Bait	Esa	餌
Shallow place	Asai tokoro	浅い所
Deep place	Fukai tokoro	深い所
High surf	Nami ga takai	波が高い
Rapid stream	Kyuuryuu	急流

	ENGLISH	ROMANIZED JAPANESE	JAPANESE
788	Do you like water sports?	Marin supootsu wa osuki desu ka?	マリンスポーツはお好きですか。
789	Golf is the most popular sport.	Gorufu wa ichiban sakanna supootsu desu.	ゴルフは一番さかんなスポーツです。
790	Surfing is popular now.	Ima, saafin ga hayatte imasu.	今、サーフィンがはやっています。
791	It's a traditional sport of this country.	Kono kuni no dentootekina supootsu desu.	この国の伝統的なスポーツです。
792	It's a sport that can be enjoyed by both young and old people.	Toshiyori mo wakai hito mo tanoshimeru supootsu desu.	年寄りも若い人も楽しめるスポーツです。
793	It's the season for cricket now.	Ima, kuriketto no shiizun desu.	今、クリケットのシーズンです。
794	The World Tennis Championship is being held here.	Koko de tenisu no sekai senshuken taikai o yatte imasu.	ここでテニスの世界選手権大会をやっています。
795	It's necessary to book.	Yoyaku ga hitsuyoo desu.	予約が必要です。

	ENGLISH	ROMANIZED JAPANESE	JAPANESE
796	We do not take bookings.	Yoyaku wa uketsukemasen.	予約は受け付けません。
797	You cannot book without an introduction from a member.	Kurabu kaiin no shookai ga naito yoyaku dekimasen.	クラブ会員の紹介がないと予約できません。
798	How many of you are there?	Nanmei desu ka?	何名ですか。
799	Have you a Japanese membership card with you?	Nihon no kaiinshoo o omochi desu ka?	日本の会員証をお持ちですか。
800	The weekend is very busy.	Shuumatsu wa konde imasu.	週末は混んでいます。
801	Friday is booked out.	Kin'yoobi wa ippai desu.	金曜日はいっぱいです。
802	Saturdays are for members only.	Doyoobi wa menbaa nomi desu.	土曜日はメンバーのみです。
803	Tuesday is available.	Kayoobi wa suite imasu.	火曜日はすいています。
804	Please wait for about half an hour.	Sanjuppun hodo matte kudasai.	30分ほど待って下さい。
805	We'll call your number over the loudspeaker.	Bangoo o supiikaa de yobimasu.	番号をスピーカーで呼びます。

172

806	Please write the group name and the number of people.	Guruupumei to ninzuu o kaite kudasai.	グループ名と人数を書いて下さい。
807	We'll send someone to get you.	Kakari no mono ga mukae ni kimasu.	係の者が迎えに来ます。
808	We open at 7 in the morning.	Asa shichiji ni akimasu.	朝7時に開きます。
809	We close at 9 in the evening.	Yoru kuji ni shimarimasu.	夜9時に閉まります。
810	They might sell it at the kiosk.	Baiten de utte irukamo shiremasen.	売店で売っているかもしれません。
811	We don't have shoes for hire.	Kashigutsu wa arimasen.	貸靴はありません。
812	What is your size?	Saizu wa ikutsu desu ka?	サイズはいくつですか。
813	We don't have any smaller size than this.	Kore yori chiisai saizu wa arimasen.	これより小さいサイズはありません。
814	Those shoes are not allowed.	Kono kutsu wa kinjirarete imasu.	この靴は禁じられています。
815	Please return them by 5 o'clock.	Goji made ni kaeshite kudasai.	5時までに返して下さい。

	ENGLISH	ROMANIZED JAPANESE	JAPANESE
816	We don't have caddies.	Kyadii wa imasen.	キャディーはいません。
817	This is the best beach for swimming.	Kaisuiyoku niwa saiteki no kaigan desu.	海水浴には最適の海岸です。
818	Please swim at the patrolled beach.	Kanshi'in no iru tokoro de oyoide kudasai.	監視員のいるところで泳いで下さい。
819	Please stay within the area where swimming is permitted.	Shitei sareta yuuei kuiki no soto ewa denaide kudasai.	指定された遊泳区域の外へは出ないで下さい。
820	Are you a good swimmer?	Oyogi wa tokui desu ka?	泳ぎは得意ですか。
821	Is this the first time you've tried diving?	Daibingu wa hajimete desu ka?	ダイビングは初めてですか。
822	There's special coaching available for beginners.	Shoshinsha yoo no kooshuu ga arimasu.	初心者用の講習があります。
823	It depends on the weather.	Tenkoo shidai desu.	天候次第です。
824	With today's bad weather, it won't be safe.	Kyoo wa tenki ga warukute, anzen dewa arimasen.	今日は天気が悪くて安全ではありません。

	ENGLISH	ROMANIZED JAPANESE	JAPANESE
825	You had better not go.	Yameta hoo ga ii desu.	やめた方がいいです。
826	It's dangerous after the heavy rain.	Ooame no ato wa abunai desu.	大雨のあとは、あぶないです。
827	You can hire all the fishing gear you need.	Tsuri doogu wa min'na kariraremasu.	釣り道具はみんな借りられます。
828	Bait is sold at the store near the pier.	Esa wa sanbashi no soba no mise de utte imasu.	餌は桟橋のそばの店で売っています。
829	The rental charge for a boat is $120.	Fune no rentaruryoo wa hyaku-nijuudoru desu.	船のレンタル料は 120 ドルです。
830	Are you interested in off-shore fishing or fishing from the beach?	Okizuri desu ka, isozuri desu ka?	沖釣りですか。磯釣りですか。
831	It's about 20 metres deep.	Mizu no fukasa wa nijuu meetoru gurai desu.	水の深さは20メートルぐらいです。
832	Did you catch a lot?	Takusan tsuremashita ka?	たくさん釣れましたか。

	ENGLISH	ROMANIZED JAPANESE	JAPANESE
833	The common catch around here is mackerel.	Konohen dewa aji ga yoku tsuremasu.	この辺ではアジがよく釣れます。
834	You are not allowed to take home small fish.	Chiisai sakana wa mochi kaeremasen.	小さい魚は持ち帰れません。
835	A licence is needed for freshwater fishing.	Kawa de tsuru niwa raisensu ga hitsuyoo desu.	川で釣るには、ライセンスが必要です。
836	Mountain rivers and lakes are full of trout.	Yama'ai no kawa ya mizuumi dewa masu ga tsuremasu.	山合いの川や湖では、マスが釣れます。

18 Theatre and show

[1] See also 13. At the restaurant: Taking a booking.

ENGLISH	ROMANIZED JAPANESE	JAPANESE
Theatre	Gekijoo	劇場
Plays	Geki	劇
Opera	Opera	オペラ
Ballet	Baree	バレー
Music	Ongaku	音楽
Concert	Ongakukai	音楽会
Concert hall	Konsaatohooru	コンサートホール
Outdoor music bowl	Yagai ongakudoo	野外音楽堂
Classical music	Kurashikku	クラシック
Symphony (orchestra)	Kookyoogaku (dan)/Ookesutora	交響楽（団）、オーケストラ
Choir (group)	Gasshoo (dan)	合唱（団）
Singer	Kashu	歌手
Pianist	Pianisuto	ピアニスト
Conductor	Shikisha	指揮者
World-famous	Sekaiteki ni yuumeina	世界的に有名な
Wonderful	Subarashii	すばらしい
Musical (show)	Myuujikaru	ミュージカル

178

ENGLISH	ROMANIZED JAPANESE	JAPANESE
Theatre restaurant	Dinaashoo no resutoran	ディナーショーのレストラン
Movie	Eiga	映画
(Movie) theatre	Eigakan	映画館
Performance	Jooen	上演
Inquiry	Toiawase	問い合わせ
Ticket	Kippu/Ken	切符、券
Ticket office	Kippu uriba	切符売場
Entrance fee	Nyuujooryoo	入場料
Free of charge	Muryoo	無料
Student concession	Gakusei waribiki	学生割引き
Door sales	Toojitsuken	当日券
Matinee	Machine	マチネ
Booking	Yoyaku	予約
Booked out	Urikire	売切れ
Seat	Seki	席
Stalls	Ikkaiseki	1 階席
Circle	Nikaiseki	2 階席

Theatre and show

ENGLISH	ROMANIZED JAPANESE	JAPANESE
Balcony	Sangaiseki	3階席
Best seat	Tokutooseki	特等席
Centre seat	Shoomenseki	正面席
Right side	Migigawa	右側
Left side	Hidarigawa	左側
～ row	～ retsume	～列目
Stage	Butai	舞台
Auditorium	Joonai	場内
Prohibited	Kinshi	禁止
Intermission	Kyuukei jikan	休憩時間
Change of scene	Makuai	幕合
Usher	An'naigakari	案内係
Entrance	Iriguchi	入口
Exit	Deguchi	出口
Restaurant	Shokudoo/Resutoran	食堂、レストラン
Snacks	Keishoku/Sunakku	軽食、スナック

	ENGLISH	ROMANIZED JAPANESE	JAPANESE
837	Would you like to book for the ballet?	Baree no yoyaku desu ka?	バレーの予約ですか。
838	I'll make an inquiry by telephone.	Denwa de kiite agemashoo.	電話で聞いてあげましょう。
839	There will be no performance of ballet tomorrow.	Ashita wa baree no jooen wa arimasen.	あしたはバレーの上演はありません。
840	The opera will be on, though.	Opera nara yatte imasu.	オペラならやっています。
841	Do you like opera?	Opera wa osuki desu ka?	オペラはお好きですか。
842	He/She is a world-famous opera singer.	Sekaiteki ni yuumeina opera kashu desu.	世界的に有名なオペラ歌手です。
843	Which would you like, stalls or circle?	Ikkaiseki to nikaiseki to dochira ga ii desu ka?	1階席と2階席と、どちらがいいですか。
844	The circle would be better to see a ballet.	Baree niwa nikaiseki no hooga ii deshoo.	バレーには2階席の方がいいでしょう。
845	We have sold out of stalls.	Ikkaiseki wa urikire desu.	1階席は売り切れです。

	ENGLISH	ROMANIZED JAPANESE	JAPANESE
846	We have only this section of the circle left.	Nikaiseki no kono basho shika nokotte imasen.	２階席のこの場所しか残っていません。
847	It's the second row, in the centre of the circle.	Nikai no shoomenseki no niretsume desu.	２階の正面席の２列目です。
848	It's a seat close to the stage.	Butai ni chikai seki desu.	舞台に近い席です。
849	We still have some seats.	Mada seki wa arimasu.	まだ席はあります。
850	There is a matinee as well.	Machine mo arimasu.	マチネもあります。
851	There will also be tickets sold at the door.	Toojitsuken mo arimasu.	当日券もあります。
852	How many tickets would you like?	Kippu wa nanmai desu ka?	切符は何枚ですか。
853	Please leave your umbrella at the cloakroom.	Kasa wa kurooku ni azukete kudasai.	傘はクロークに預けて下さい。
854	May I see your ticket(s), please?	Kippu o haiken shimasu.	切符を拝見します。

	ENGLISH	ROMANIZED JAPANESE	JAPANESE
855	I'll show you to your seat(s). Please come this way.	Seki ni goan'nai shimasu. Doozo kochirani.	席にご案内します。どうぞ こちらに。
856	Your seat is at the side of this row.	Kono retsu no hashi desu.	この列の端です。
857	Excuse me Sir/Madam, you are in the wrong seat.	Okyakusama seki ga machigatte imasu.	お客様、席が間違っていま す。
858	The performance has already started. You cannot go in now.	Moo hajimatte imasu node hairemasen.	もう始まっていますので、 入れません。
859	Please wait a little while.	Shibaraku omachi kudasai.	しばらくお待ち下さい。
860	Eating and drinking are not permitted in the auditorium.	Joonai deno inshoku wa goenryo kudasai.	場内での飲食はご遠慮下さ い。
861	Would you like a programme?	Puroguramu wa ikaga desu ka?	プログラムはいかがですか。
862	The doors will be open at 7 o'clock.	Kaijoo wa shichiji desu.	開場は7時です。
863	The performance will begin at half past 7.	Kaien wa shichiji han desu.	開演は7時半です。

	ENGLISH	ROMANIZED JAPANESE	JAPANESE
864	There are 2 intermissions.	Kyuukei ga nikai arimasu.	休憩が2回あります。
865	There is no intermission.	Kyuukei nashi desu.	休憩なしです。
866	It will finish at half past 10.	Juuji han ni owarimasu.	10時半に終わります。
867	You can have dinner whilst watching the show.	Shoo o minagara shokuji ga dekimasu.	ショーを見ながら食事ができます。
868	The next floor show is at 8 o'clock.	Tsugi no furoashoo wa hachiji desu.	次のフロアショーは8時です。
869	The show goes for 1 hour.	Shoo wa ichijikan desu.	ショーは1時間です。
870	You can dance after the show.	Shoo no ato odoremasu.	ショーのあと踊れます。
871	Please sing along with me.	Doozo issho ni utatte kudasai.	どうぞ一緒に歌って下さい。

19 Climate and clothing

185

Climate and clothing

ENGLISH	ROMANIZED JAPANESE	JAPANESE
Climate	Kikoo	気候
Season	Kisetsu	季節
Weather	Tenki	天気
Weather forecast	Tenki yohoo	天気予報
Temperature	Kion	気温
Maximum	Saikoo	最高
Average temperature	Heikin kion	平均気温
― degrees	― do	～度
Below zero	Hyootenka	氷点下
Cold (weather)	Samui	寒い
Cool (weather)	Suzushii	涼しい
Warm	Atatakai	暖い
Hot	Atsui	暑い
Humid	Mushiatsui	むし暑い
Mild	Odayaka	おだやか
Dry	Kansoo shite iru	乾燥している
Pleasant	Sugoshi yasui	過ごしやすい

ENGLISH	ROMANIZED JAPANESE	JAPANESE
Harsh	Kibishii	きびしい
Morning	Asa	朝
During the day	Hiruma	昼間
Night	Yoru	夜
Air	Kuuki	空気
Sky	Sora	空
Sun	Taiyoo	太陽
Moon	Tsuki	月
Star	Hoshi	星
Clear	Hare	晴れ
Cloudy	Kumori	曇り
Rain	Ame	雨
Shower	Niwakaame	にわか雨
Heavy rain	Ooame	大雨
Wind	Kaze	風
Snow	Yuki	雪
Storm	Arashi	嵐

Climate and clothing

ENGLISH	ROMANIZED JAPANESE	JAPANESE
Clothing	Fukusoo	服装
(Western) Clothes	Yoofuku	洋服
Men's suits	Sebiro	背広
Casual clothes	Kajuaru na fukusoo	カジュアルな服装
Coat	Uwagi/Kooto	上衣、コート
Sweater/Jumper	Seetaa	セーター
Business shirt	Waishatsu	ワイシャツ
Short sleeves	Hansode	半袖
Long sleeves	Nagasode	長袖
Open-necked shirt	Kaikin shatsu	開襟シャツ
Change of clothes	Kigae	着替え
Underwear	Shitagi	下着
Socks	Kutsushita/Sokkusu	靴下、ソックス
Sports shoes	Undoogutsu	運動靴
Walking shoes	Arukiyasui kutsu	歩きやすい靴
Hat/Cap	Booshi	帽子

	ENGLISH	ROMANIZED JAPANESE	JAPANESE
872	It's spring now.	Ima, haru desu.	今、春です。
873	This is the best time of the year.	Ima ga ichiban ii kisetsu desu.	今が一番いい季節です。
874	The maximum temperature in summer is about 30°C.	Natsu no saikoo kion wa sanjuudo gurai desu.	夏の最高気温は30度位です。
875	The mornings and nights are cool, even if it's hot during the day.	Hiruma wa atsukutemo, asa to yoru wa hiemasu.	昼間は暑くても、朝と夜は冷えます。
876	The climate here is dry.	Kono tochi no kikoo wa kansoo shite imasu.	この土地の気候は乾燥しています。
877	We have a lot of rain in autumn.	Aki ni takusan ame ga furimasu.	秋にたくさん雨が降ります。
878	It doesn't snow, even in winter.	Fuyu demo yuki wa furimasen.	冬でも雪は降りません。
879	The average temperature in winter is 6°C.	Fuyo no heikin kion wa rokudo desu.	冬の平均気温は6度です。

	ENGLISH	ROMANIZED JAPANESE	JAPANESE
880	Winter is harsh, with the temperature dropping to 10°C below zero.	Fuyu wa hyootenka juudo de kibishii desu.	冬は氷点下10度できびしいです。
881	According to the weather forecast, it will be good weather today.	Tenki yohoo dewa, kyoo wa ii tenki desu.	天気予報では、今日はいい天気です。
882	It should clear up in the afternoon.	Gogo kara hareru deshoo.	午後から晴れるでしょう。
883	There will be showers from time to time.	Tokidoki niwakaame ga arimasu.	時々にわか雨があります。
884	It would be better to take an umbrella with you.	Kasa o motte itta hoo ga ii desu.	傘を持って行った方がいいです。
885	The wind is strong as it's on the beach.	Kaigan desu kara kaze ga tsuyoi desu.	海岸ですから、風が強いです。
886	Perhaps the weather will improve tomorrow.	Ashita wa kitto ii tenki deshoo.	あしたはきっといい天気でしょう。
887	Tomorrow will be clear, but cloudy at times.	Ashita wa haretari kumottari desu.	あしたは、晴れたりくもったりです。

	ENGLISH	ROMANIZED JAPANESE	JAPANESE
888	The rain should stop soon.	Ame wa moosugu yamu deshoo.	雨はもうすぐやむでしょう。
889	They say that tomorrow will be colder than today.	Ashita wa kyoo yori samui soo desu.	あしたは今日より寒いそうです。
890	We rarely have heavy rain like this.	Kon'na ooame wa mezurashii desu.	こんな大雨はめずらしいです。
891	You had better not go out as there is a storm.	Arashi desu kara, gaishutsu shinai hoo ga ii desu.	嵐ですから外出しない方がいいです。
892	It's going to hail. Be careful.	Hyoo ga futte kimasu. Ki o tsukete kudasai.	ひょうが降ってきます。気をつけて下さい。
893	What you are wearing is all right.	Sono fukusoo de daijoobu desu.	その服装で大丈夫です。
894	Do you want to get any clothes out of your suitcase?	Suutsukeesu kara yoofuku o dashimasu ka?	スーツケースから洋服を出しますか。
895	Do you have anything to wear on top?	Uwagi o motte imasu ka?	上衣を持っていますか。
896	Please come with warm clothing.	Samukunai fukusoo de kite kudasai.	寒くない服装で来て下さい。
897	Casual clothes are acceptable at this restaurant.	Kono resutoran wa, kajuaruna fukusoo de ii desu.	このレストランは、カジュアルな服装でいいです。

	ENGLISH	ROMANIZED JAPANESE	JAPANESE
898	Any clothes are right, except for jeans.	Jiinzu igai nara nan demo ii desu.	ジーンズ以外なら何でもいいです。
899	Open-necked shirts or T-shirts are not allowed.	Kaikin shatsu ya tiishatsu wa dame desu.	開襟シャツやTシャツは駄目です。
900	You must wear a tie.	Nekutai o shinakereba ikemasen.	ネクタイをしなければいけません。
901	It'll be handy if you carry a raincoat with you.	Reinkooto o motte iruto benri desu.	レインコートを持っていると便利です。
902	Long sleeves would be better.	Nagasode no hoo ga ii desu.	長袖の方がいいです。
903	Discos will not let you in without proper shoes.	Chantoshita kutsu de naito, disuko ni hairemasen.	ちゃんとした靴でないと、ディスコに入れません。
904	Please wear walking shoes.	Arukiyasui kutsu o haite kudasai.	歩きやすい靴をはいて下さい。
905	Sandals are slippery and dangerous.	Sandaru wa suberiyasukute, abunai desu.	サンダルはすべりやすくてあぶないです。
906	Please don't go out of your room wearing slippers.	Surippa de heya no soto ni denaide kudasai.	スリッパで部屋の外に出ないで下さい。

20 Illness and injuries

Illness and injuries

ENGLISH	ROMANIZED JAPANESE	JAPANESE
Illness	Byooki	病気
Injury	Kega	けが
Doctor	Isha	医者
Hospital	Byooin	病院
Hospitalization	Nyuuin	入院
Drug store/Chemist	Yakkyoku	薬局
Medicine	Kusuri	薬
Prescription	Shohoosen	処方せん
Feeling sick	Kibun ga warui	気分が悪い
Feel like vomiting	Hakike	吐き気
Hurt/Painful	Itai	痛い
Dull pain	Dontsuu	鈍痛
Sharp pain	Surudoi itami	鋭い痛み
Difficulty breathing	Ikigurushii	息苦しい
Indigestion/Heartburn	Muneyake	胸やけ
Cough	Seki	せき
Dizziness	Memai	めまい

ENGLISH	ROMANIZED JAPANESE	JAPANESE
Fever	Netsu	熱
Skin	Hifu	皮膚
Spots (eczema)	Shisshin	湿疹
Diarrhoea	Geri	下痢
Constipation	Benpi	便秘
Cut	Kizuguchi	傷口
Cold, a	Kaze	風邪
Sprain	Nenza	捻挫
Insect bite	**Mushi sasare**	**虫刺され**
Symptoms	Shoojoo	症状
Urine	Nyoo	尿
Injection	Chuusha	注射
X-ray	Rentogen	レントゲン
Allergic	Arerugii	アレルギー
Penicillin	Penishirin	ペニシリン
Antibiotics	Koosei Busshitsu	抗生物質
Germ	Baikin	ばい菌

Illness and injuries

ENGLISH	ROMANIZED JAPANESE	JAPANESE
Breath	Iki	息
Blood type	Ketsuekigata	血液型
Thermometer (clinical)	Taionkei	体温計
Sleeping pill	Suimin'yaku	睡眠薬
Pain killer	Chintsuuzai	鎮痛剤
Medicine for stomach upsets	Ichooyaku	胃腸薬
Disinfectant	Shoodokuyaku	消毒薬
Compress, a	Shippu	湿布
Bandage	Hootai	ほうたい
Every 4 hours	Yojikan oki	4時間おき
After meals	Shokugo	食後
一 tablet	一 joo	〜錠
Rest	Ansei	安静
Medical examination	Shinsatsu	診察
Medical certificate	Shindansho	診断書
Travel insurance	Ryokoo hoken	旅行保険

	ENGLISH	ROMANIZED JAPANESE	JAPANESE
907	Are you not feeling well?	Gokibun demo warui no desu ka?	ご気分でも悪いのですか。
908	Shall we stop to rest a moment?	Sukoshi yasumimashoo ka?	少し休みましょうか。
909	Shall I open the window?	Mado o akemashoo ka?	窓を開けましょうか。
910	Let's buy some medicine at the drug store.	Yakkyoku de kusuri o kaimashoo.	薬局で薬を買いましょう。
911	Do you want me to call a doctor?	Isha o yobimashoo ka?	医者を呼びましょうか。
912	The doctor will come to see you at 7 o'clock.	Isha wa shichiji ni kimasu.	医者は7時に来ます。
913	Please wait in your room.	Heya de matte ite kudasai.	部屋で待っていて下さい。
914	Would you like a band-aid?	Bandoeido o agemashoo ka?	バンドエイドをあげましょうか。
915	What would you like to eat?	Nani o meshiagarimasu ka?	何を召し上がりますか。

	ENGLISH	ROMANIZED JAPANESE	JAPANESE
916	Have a good rest.	Yukkuri yasunde kudasai.	ゆっくり休んで下さい。
917	Look after yourself.	Doozo odaijini.	どうぞお大事に。
918	I hope you get better soon.	Hayaku genki ni natte kudasai.	早く元気になって下さい。
919	Are you feeling better?	Moo yoku narimashita ka?	もうよくなりましたか。
920	I'm so glad that you got better.	Genki ni natte yokatta desu ne.	元気になって良かったですね。
921	Is your throat sore?	Nodo ga itai no desu ka?	のどが痛いのですか。
922	Have you got a cough?	Seki ga demasu ka?	せきが出ますか。
923	Is your nose blocked?	Hana ga tsumarimasu ka?	鼻がつまりますか。
924	Have you a fever?	Netsu ga arimasu ka?	熱がありますか。
925	Is it septic (festered)?	Kanoo shite imasu ka?	化膿していますか。
926	I'll go and buy your medicine with this prescription.	Kono shohoosen de, watashi ga kusuri o katte kite agemasu.	この処方せんで私が薬を買って来て上げます。

	ENGLISH	ROMANIZED JAPANESE	JAPANESE
927	You cannot buy it without a prescription.	Shohoosen ga naito kaemasen.	処方せんがないと買えません。
928	You had better see a doctor.	Isha ni mite moratta hoo ga ii desu.	医者にみてもらった方がいいです。
929	What can I do for you?	Doo nasaimashita ka?	どうなさいましたか。
930	Since when have you had these symptoms?	Itsukara sono shoojoo ga arimasu ka?	いつからその症状がありますか。
931	Where does it hurt?	Doko ga itai desu ka?	どこが痛いですか。
932	Does it hurt all the time?	Zutto itai desu ka?	ずっと痛いですか。
933	Have you got a cold?	Kaze o hiite imasu ka?	風邪をひいていますか。
934	Are you pregnant?	Ninshin shite imasu ka?	妊娠していますか。
935	Do you have any chronic illness?	Jibyoo ga arimasu ka?	持病がありますか。
936	Have you ever had pneumonia?	Haien o shita koto ga arimasu ka?	肺炎をしたことがありますか。

	ENGLISH	ROMANIZED JAPANESE	JAPANESE
937	What is your blood type?	Ketsuekigata wa nan desu ka?	血液型は何ですか。
938	Are you allergic to penicillin?	Penishirin ni kyozetsu han'noo o okoshimasu ka?	ペニシリンに拒絶反応を起こしますか。
939	Please hold your breath for a second.	Iki o tomete kudasai.	息をとめて下さい。
940	I'll give you antibiotics.	Koosei busshitsu no kusuri o agemashoo.	抗生物質の薬をあげましょう。
941	Virulent influenza is going around.	Akusei no infuruenza ga hayatte imasu.	悪性のインフルエンザがはやっています。
942	It is an ordinary cold.	Tada no kaze desu.	ただの風邪です。
943	You seem to be overtired.	Tsukare sugi no yoo desu.	疲れ過ぎのようです。
944	You must not drink alcohol.	Arukooru o nondewa ikemasen.	アルコールを飲んではいけません。
945	Do not eat any oily foods.	Aburakkoi mono o tabetewa ikemasen.	油っこい物を食べてはいけません。

	ENGLISH	ROMANIZED JAPANESE	JAPANESE
946	You can have a bath.	Ofuro ni haittemo kamaimasen.	お風呂に入ってもかまいません。
947	You must stay quiet.	Ansei ni shiteite kudasai.	安静にしていて下さい。
948	You need plenty of rest.	Juubun yasumanakutewa ikemasen.	十分休まなくてはいけません。
949	Take 2 tablets after meals.	Kusuri wa shokugo nijoo nonde kudasai.	薬は食後2錠飲んで下さい。
950	Take them until they're all finished.	Zenbu owaru made fukuyoo shite kudasai.	全部終わるまで服用して下さい。
951	You cannot continue your trip.	Ryokoo wa tsuzukerare masen.	旅行は続けられません。
952	You shouldn't move vigorously.	Amari kappatsu ni ugoitewa ikemasen.	余り活発に動いてはいけません。
953	You must stay in hospital.	Nyuuin shinakereba narimasen.	入院しなければなりません。
954	This is emergency treatment until you return to Japan.	Kikoku made no ookyuu teate desu.	帰国までの応急手当です。

	ENGLISH	ROMANIZED JAPANESE	JAPANESE
955	Have a doctor check you in Japan.	Nihon de isha ni mite moratte kudasai.	日本で医者にみてもらって下さい。

21 Accidents and emergency

[1] See also 3. Arrival and Customs: Lost luggage.
[2] See also 7. At the bank: Lost travellers cheques.

ENGLISH	ROMANIZED JAPANESE	JAPANESE
Accident	Jiko	事故
Things left behind	Wasuremono	忘れ物
Lost property	Funshitsu	紛失
Lost property office	Ishitsubutsu gakari	遺失物係
Damaged/Broken	Hason	破損
Form	Yooshi	用紙
Features	Tokuchoo	特徴
Name tag	Nafuda	名礼
Safe-keeping/Storage	Hokan	保管
Contact	Renraku	連絡
Name	Namae	名前
Address	Juusho	住所
Signature	Shomei/Sain	署名、サイン
Telephone number	Denwa bangoo	電話番号
Compensation	Benshoo	弁償
Receipt	Ryooshuusho	領収書
Refund	Henkin	返金

ENGLISH	ROMANIZED JAPANESE	JAPANESE
Return of goods	Henpin	返品
Exchange	Kookan	交換
Repair	Shuuri	修理
Person in charge	Kakari no hito	係の人
Out of order	Koshoochuu	故障中
Black-out/Power cut	Teiden	停電
Fire	Kaji	火事
Emergency exit	Hijooguchi	非常口
Dangerous	Abunai	あぶない
Theft	Toonan	盗難
Contents	Nakami	中味
Ambulance	Kyuukyuusha	救急車
Doctor	Isha	医者
Policeman	Keikan	警官
Police station	Keisatsu	警察
Police report on the theft	Toonan shoomeisho	盗難証明書
Police report on the accident	Jiko shoomeisho	事故証明書

ENGLISH	ROMANIZED JAPANESE	JAPANESE
Damage (by accident)	Songai	損害
Motor-car driving licence	Jidoosha unten menkyoshoo	自動車運転免許証
Parking infringement	Chuusha ihan	駐車違反
Speed limit violation	Supiido ihan	スピード違反
Drink driving	Inshu unten	飲酒運転
Fine, a	Bakkin	罰金
Mail/Post	Yuubin	郵便
Notice/Advice	Tsuuchi	通知
Court	Saibansho	裁判所
Document	Shorui	書類
Embassy	Taishikan	大使館
Consulate	Ryoojikan	領事館
Re-issue	Saihakkoo	再発行
Procedure	Tetsuzuki	手続き
Valid/Effective	Yuukoo	有効
Invalid	Mukoo	無効

	ENGLISH	ROMANIZED JAPANESE	JAPANESE
956	What have you lost?	Nani o nakushita no desu ka?	何をなくしたのですか。
957	When did you lose it?	Itsu nakushimashita ka?	いつなくしましたか。
958	Where did you lose it?	Doko ni wasuremashita ka?	どこに忘れましたか。
959	Please go to the lost property office.	Ishitsubutsu gakari ni itte kudasai.	遺失物係に行って下さい。
960	It hasn't come here.	Koko niwa todoite imasen.	ここには届いていません。
961	Please describe the features of the bag.	Kaban no tokuchoo o itte kudasai.	かばんの特徴を言って下さい。
962	We will keep it here when it's found.	Mitsukattara koko de hokan shimasu.	見つかったらここで保管します。
963	We'll contact you if it's found.	Mitsukattara renraku shimasu.	見つかったら連絡します。
964	Please ring this number tomorrow.	Ashita, kono bangoo ni denwa shite kudasai.	明日、この番号に電話して下さい。
965	Please write your telephone number here.	Koko ni renrakusaki o kaite kudasai.	ここに連絡先を書いて下さい。

	ENGLISH	ROMANIZED JAPANESE	JAPANESE
966	Please write your name and address.	Juusho to namae o kaite kudasai.	住所と名前を書いて下さい。
967	Please sign here.	Koko ni shomei o onegai shimasu.	ここに署名をお願いします。
968	We can't give you a refund without a receipt.	Ryooshuusho ga naito henkin dekimasen.	領収書がないと返金できません。
969	You cannot return this article.	Kono shinamono wa henpin dekimasen.	この品物は返品できません。
970	You may exchange it for something else.	Hoka no mono to kookan shitemo kamaimasen.	外の物と交換してもかまいません。
971	We'll have it repaired without delay.	Suguni shuuri shimasu.	すぐに修理します。
972	The person in charge will be here immediately.	Suguni kakari no mono ga kimasu.	すぐに係の者が来ます。
973	The elevator is out of order.	Erebeetaa ga koshoochuu desu.	エレベーターが故障中です。

	ENGLISH	ROMANIZED JAPANESE	JAPANESE
974	You cannot use electrical appliances due to the power cut.	Teiden no tame, denkikigu ga tsukaemasen.	停電のため、電気器具が使えません。
975	We apologize for the inconvenience.	Gomeiwaku o kakete, mooshiwake arimasen.	ご迷惑をかけて申し訳ありません。
976	There's a fire.	Kaji desu.	火事です。
977	Please do not use the elevator.	Erebeetaa wa tsukawanaide kudasai.	エレベーターは使わないで下さい。
978	The emergency exit is that way.	Hijooguchi wa achira desu.	非常口はあちらです。
979	You are not in danger.	Abunakunai desu.	あぶなくないです。
980	Please get clear without panicking.	Ki o ochitsukete nigete kudasai.	気を落ちつけて逃げて下さい。
981	Where were you robbed?	Doko de toonan ni aimashita ka?	どこで盗難にあいましたか。
982	What did you have stolen?	Nani o nusumaremashita ka?	何を盗まれましたか。

	ENGLISH	ROMANIZED JAPANESE	JAPANESE
983	What was in it?	Naka ni don'na mono ga haitte imashita ka?	中にどんな物が入っていましたか。
984	The hotel does not accept liability.	Hoteru no sekinin niwa narimasen.	ホテルの責任にはなりません。
985	Please talk into this.	Kore o kuchi ni atete nani ka itte kudasai.	これを口に当てて何か言って下さい。
986	The ambulance will be here soon.	Suguni kyuukyuusha ga kimasu.	すぐに救急車が来ます。
987	Please don't move.	Ugokanaide kudasai.	動かないで下さい。
988	Don't worry. It's not a serious injury.	Daijoobu desu. Taishita kega dewa arimasen.	大丈夫です。たいした怪我ではありません。
989	A doctor and an interpreter will come shortly.	Isha to tsuuyaku ga ima kimasu.	医者と通訳が今来ます。
990	Are you covered by any travel insurance?	Ryokoo hoken ni kanyuu shite imasu ka?	旅行保険に加入していますか。
991	Do you want to report it to the police?	Keisatsu ni todokemasu ka?	警察に届けますか。

	ENGLISH	ROMANIZED JAPANESE	JAPANESE
992	You had better get a police report on the theft.	Keisatsu no toonan shoomeisho o moratta hoo ga ii desu.	警察の盗難証明書をもらった方がいいです。
993	You'll need a police report on the accident.	Keisatsu no jiko shoomeisho ga hitsuyoo desu.	警察の事故証明書が必要です。
994	You have to pay a $100 fine.	Hyakudoru no bakkin desu.	100ドルの罰金です。
995	You may pay it now.	Ima harattemo ii desu.	今払ってもいいです。
996	You are required to pay within 28 days.	Nijuuhachi nichi inai ni harawanakereba narimasen.	28日以内に払わなければなりません。
997	The notice will be posted to you.	Yuubin de tsuuchi shimasu.	郵便で通知します。
998	You must go to the police station.	Keisatsu ni ikanakereba narimasen.	警察に行かなければなりません。
999	You must complete the necessary procedure at a consulate.	Ryoojikan de tetsuzuki o toranakereba narimasen.	領事館で手続きを取らなければなりません。

	ENGLISH	ROMANIZED JAPANESE	JAPANESE
1000	We'll arrange an interpreter for you.	Tsuuyaku wa kochira de tehai shimasu.	通訳は、こちらで手配します。

Useful verbs

English	Affirmative present/future **-masu**	Negative present/future **-masen**	Form for request **-te kudasai**
accept (receive)	itadakimasu	itadakimasen	-
arrive	tsukimasu	tsukimasen	-
be (subject is a thing)	arimasu	arimasen	-
be (subject is a person)	imasu	imasen	ite kudasai
be able	dekimasu	dekimasen	-
be crowded	komimasu	komimasen	-
be wrong	chigaimasu	chigaimasen	-
beg a favour	onegaishimasu	onegaishimasen	onegaishite kudasai

Useful verbs

English	Affirmative present/future -masu	Negative present/future -masen	Form for request -te kudasai
bring (a thing)	mottekimasu	mottekimasen	mottekite kudasai
buy	kaimasu	kaimasen	katte kudasai
close/shut	shimemasu	shimemasen	shimete kudasai
come	kimasu	kimasen	kite kudasai
deliver	todokemasu	todokemasen	todokete kudasai
do	shimasu	shimasen	shite kudasai
drink	nomimasu	nomimasen	nonde kudasai
eat	tabemasu	tabemasen	tabete kudasai
enter	hairimasu	hairimasen	haitte kudasai
(it) finishes	owarimasu	owarimasen	-
get off (a train)	orimasu	orimasen	orite kudasai

English	Affirmative present/future **-masu**	Negative present/future **-masen**	Form for request **-te kudasai**
give	agemasu	agemasen	agete kudasai
go	ikimasu	ikimasen	itte kudasai
have	arimasu	arimasen	-
have (carry)	mochimasu	mochimasen	motte kudasai
leave (depart)	demasu	demasen	dete kudasai
listen	kikimasu	kikimasen	kiite kudasai
make	tsukurimasu	tsukurimasen	tsukutte kudasai
meet/see (a person)	aimasu	aimasen	atte kudasai
open	akemasu	akemasen	akete kudasai
push	oshimasu	oshimasen	oshite kudasai
read	yomimasu	yomimasen	yonde kudasai

English	Affirmative present/future -masu	Negative present/future -masen	Form for request -te kudasai
receive	uketorimasu	uketorimasen	uketotte kudasai
return (go back)	kaerimasu	kaerimasen	kaette kudasai
ride	norimasu	norimasen	notte kudasai
say	iimasu	iimasen	itte kudasai
see (look)	mimasu	mimasen	mite kudasai
sell	urimasu	urimasen	utte kudasai
send	okurimasu	okurimasen	okutte kudasai
show	misemasu	misemasen	misete kudasai
sit down	suwarimasu	suwarimasen	suwatte kudasai
smoke	suimasu	suimasen	sutte kudasai
(it) stops	tomarimasu	tomarimasen	tomatte kudasai

	Affirmative present/future **-masu**	Negative present/future **-masen**	Form for request **-te kudasai**
stop (a car)	tomemasu	tomemasen	tomete kudasai
take (a picture)	torimasu	torimasen	totte kudasai
(it) takes (time)	kakarimasu	kakarimasen	-
tell (let you know)	oshiemasu	oshiemasen	oshiete kudasai
turn (the corner)	magarimasu	magarimasen	magatte kudasai
understand	wakarimasu	wakarimasen	-
use	tsukaimasu	tsukaimasen	tsukatte kudasai
wait	machimasu	machimasen	matte kudasai
walk	arukimasu	arukimasen	aruite kudasai
write	kakimasu	kakimasen	kaite kudasai

Note The Japanese language has no grammatical form for distinguishing person or number. The same form is used regardless of the subject, e.g. SUGU KIMASU (I/you/he/we/they will come soon).

Useful adjectives

ENGLISH	ROMANIZED JAPANESE	ENGLISH	ROMANIZED JAPANESE
bad	warui	dangerous	abunai
boring	tsumaranai	dark	kurai
bright	akarui	delicious	oishii
busy	isogashii	difficult	muzukashii
cheap	yasui	dirty	kitanai
clean	kirei	dislike	kirai
cold (drink)	tsumetai	early/fast	hayai
cold (weather)	samui	easy	yasashii
convenient	benri	expensive	takai
correct	tadashii	famous	yuumei

ENGLISH	ROMANIZED JAPANESE	ENGLISH	ROMANIZED JAPANESE
far	tooi	inconvenient	fuben
fast	hayai	interesting	omoshiroi
few	sukunai	kind	shinsetsu
free time/leisure	hima	large	ookii
good	ii	late	osoi
healthy	genki	light (weight)	karui
heavy	omoi	likeable/like[1]	suki
high	takai	(a) little	sukoshi
hot (spicy)	karai	lively	nigiyaka
hot (temperature)	atsui	long	nagai
hurt/sore	itai	low	hikui
important	daiji	many	ooi

[1] The verb 'to like' in Japanese conjugates as an adjective, i.e. it takes the '-desu' ending rather than the verbial '-masu' ending.

Useful adjectives

ENGLISH	ROMANIZED JAPANESE	ENGLISH	ROMANIZED JAPANESE
much	takusan	short	mijikai
narrow	semai	skilful	joozu
near	chikai	slow	osoi
new	atarashii	small	chiisai
no good/useless	dame	sour	suppai
old (an object)	furui	special	tokubetsu
pleasant	tanoshii	sweet	amai
polite	teinei	unkind	fushinsetsu
pretty	kirei	unskilful	heta
quiet	shizuka	various	iroiro
rude	shitsurei	warm	atatakai
safe	anzen	wide/spacious	hiroi
salty	shiokarai	young	wakai

Countries and languages spoken

Country	Pronunciation in Japanese	Language used
Australia	Oosutoraria	Ei-go
Austria	Oosutoria	Doitsu-go
Brazil	Burajiru	Porutogaru-go
Canada	Kanada	Ei-go/Furansu-go
China	Chuugoku	Chuugoku-go
Denmark	Denmaaku	Denmaaku-go
England	Igirisu	Ei-go
Egypt	Ejiputo	Arabia-go
France	Furansu	Furansu-go

Countries and languages spoken

Country	Pronunciation in Japanese	Language used
Germany	Doitsu	Doitsu-go
Greece	Girisha	Girisha-go
Holland	Oranda	Oranda-go
Indonesia	Indoneshia	Indoneshia-go
Italy	Itaria	Itaria-go
Japan	Nihon	Nihon-go
Korea	Kankoku	Kankoku-go
Malaysia	Mareeshia	Maree-go
New Caledonia	Nyuukaredonia	Furansu-go
New Zealand	Nyuujiirando	Ei-go
Portugal	Porutogaru	Porutogaru-go
Philippines, The	Firipin	Ei-go

Country	Pronunciation in Japanese	Language used
Russia	Roshia	Roshia-go
Singapore	Shingapooru	Ei-go/Chuugoku-go/Maree-go
Spain	Supein	Supein-go
Sweden	Sueeden	Sueeden-go
Switzerland	Suisu	Doitsu-go/Furansu-go/Itaria-go
Thailand	Tai	Tai-go
United States, The	Amerika	Ei-go

Numbers

1	ichi	11	juuichi	30	sanjuu	300	sanbyaku	4000	yonsen
2	ni	12	juuni	40	yonjuu	400	yonhyaku	5000	gosen
3	san	13	juusan	50	gojuu	500	gohyaku	6000	rokusen
4	shi/yon	14	juushi	60	rokujuu	600	roppyaku	7000	nanasen
5	go	15	juugo	70	shichijuu/ nanajuu	700	nanahyaku	8000	hassen
6	roku	16	juuroku			800	happyaku	9000	kyuusen
7	shichi/nana	17	juushichi	80	hachijuu	900	kyuuhyaku	10 000	ichiman
8	hachi	18	juuhachi	90	kyuujuu	1000	sen	100 000	juuman
9	ku/kyuu	19	juuku	100	hyaku	2000	nisen	1 000 000	hyakuman
10	juu	20	nijuu	200	nihyaku	3000	sanzen	10 000 000	issenman

How to count

† Used when counting off things and animals but not people. Though not strictly correct, this general form can be used instead of number + suffix (or 'counter').
e.g. Biiru o <u>ippon</u> desu ka? (One bottle of beer, sir?)
Biiru o <u>hitotsu</u> desu ka?

	General†	Floors	Kilometre & kilogram
1	hitotsu	ikkai	ichikiro
2	futatsu	nikai	nikiro
3	mittsu	**sangai**	sankiro
4	yottsu	yonkai	yonkiro
5	itsutsu	gokai	gokiro
6	muttsu	rokkai	rokkiro
7	nanatsu	nanakai	shichikiro/nanakiro
8	yattsu	**hachikai**	hachikiro
9	kokonotsu	kyuukai	kyuukiro
10	too	jukkai	jukkiro
11	juuichi	juuikkai	juuichikiro
12	juuni	juunikai	juunikiro
?	ikutsu	nankai	nankiro

? = How many?

Which floor?
How many floors?

How many kilometres?
How many kilograms?

How to count

	Years	People	Age
1	ichinen	hitori	issai
2	ninen	futari	nisai
3	san'nen	san'nin	sansai
4	yonen	yonin	yonsai
5	gonen	gonin	gosai
6	rokunen	rokunin	rokusai
7	shichinen/nananen	shichinin/nananin	shichisai/nanasai
8	hachinen	hachinin	hassai
9	kyuunen	kyuunin/kunin	kyuusai
10	juunen	juunin	jussai
11	juuichinen	juuichinin	juuissai
12	juuninen	juuninin	juunisai
?	nan'nen	nan'nin	nansai

? = How many years?   How many people?   How old?

	Days	Weeks	Months
1	ichinichi	isshuukan	ikkagetsu
2	futsuka	nishuukan	nikagetsu
3	mikka	sanshuukan	sankagetsu
4	yokka	yonshuukan	yonkagetsu
5	itsuka	goshuukan	gokagetsu
6	muika	rokushuukan	rokkagetsu
7	nanoka	nanashuukan	nanakagetsu
8	yooka	hasshuukan	hakkagetsu
9	kokonoka	kyuushuukan	kyuukagetsu
10	tooka	jusshuukan	jukkagetsu
11	juuichinichi	juuisshuukan	juuikkagetsu
12	juuninichi	juunishuukan	juunikagetsu
?	nan'nichi	nanshuukan	nankagetsu

? = How many days?   How many weeks?   How many months?

How to count

	Minutes	Hours	O'clock
1	ippun	ichijikan	ichiji
2	nifun	nijikan	niji
3	sanpun	sanjikan	sanji
4	yonpun	yojikan	yoji
5	gofun	gojikan	goji
6	roppun	rokujikan	rokuji
7	shichifun/nanafun	shichijikan/nanajikan	shichiji/nanaji
8	happun	hachijikan	hachiji
9	kyuufun	kujikan	kuji
10	juppun	juujikan	juuji
11	juuippun	juuichijikan	juuichiji
12	juunifun	juunijikan	juuniji
?	nanpun	nanjikan	nanji

? = How many minutes?   How many hours?   What time is it?

	Dollars	Cents	Drinks (glasses)
1	ichidoru	issento	ippai
2	nidoru	nisento	nihai
3	sandoru	sansento	sanbai
4	yondoru	yonsento	yonhai
5	godoru	gosento	gohai
6	rokudoru	rokusento	roppai
7	nanadoru/shichidoru	nanasento/shichisento	nanahai/shichihai
8	hachidoru	hassento	happai
9	kyuudoru	kyuusento	kyuuhai
10	juudoru	jussento	juppai
11	juuichidoru	juuissento	juuippai
12	juunidoru	juunisento	juunihai
?	nandoru	nansento	nanbai

? = How much?   How much?   How many glasses?

229

Names of the months

January	Ichigatsu
February	Nigatsu
March	Sangatsu
April	Shigatsu
May	Gogatsu
June	Rokugatsu
July	Shichigatsu
August	Hachigatsu
September	Kugatsu
October	Juugatsu
November	Juuichigatsu
December	Juunigatsu
?	Nangatsu

? = What month is it?

Days of the month

1	tsuitachi	11	juuichinichi	21	nijuuichi-nichi
2	futsuka	12	juuninichi	22	nijuuni-nichi
3	mikka	13	juusan'nichi	23	nijuusan-nichi
4	yokka	14	juuyokka	24	nijuuyokka
5	itsuka	15	juugonichi	25	nijuugo-nichi
6	muika	16	juurokunichi	26	nijuuroku-nichi
7	nanoka	17	juushichinichi	27	nijuushichi-nichi
8	yooka	18	juuhachinichi	28	nijuuhachi-nichi
9	kokonoka	19	juukunichi	29	nijuuku-nichi
10	tooka	20	hatsuka	30	sanjuu-nichi
				31	sanjuuichi-nichi
				?	nan'nichi

? = What is the date?

Week, month, year

last week	senshuu
this week	konshuu
next week	raishuu
last month	sengetsu
this month	kongetsu
next month	raigetsu
last year	kyonen
this year	kotoshi
next year	rainen

Seasons and locations

spring	haru		north	kita
summer	natsu		south	minami
autumn	aki		east	higashi
winter	fuyu		west	nishi

Colours

black	kuroi		pink	pinku
blue	aoi		purple	murasaki
brown	chairoi		red	akai
grey	guree		white	shiroi
green	guriin, midori		yellow	kiiroi
orange	orenji			

Days of the week

Sunday	Nichiyoobi
Monday	Getsuyoobi
Tuesday	Kayoobi
Wednesday	Suiyoobi
Thursday	Mokuyoobi
Friday	Kin' yoobi
Saturday	Doyoobi
?	Nan' yoobi

? = What day is it?

Which day?

day before yesterday	ototoi
yesterday	kinoo
today	kyoo
tomorrow	ashita
day after tomorrow	asatte

Every …

every day	mainichi
every morning	maiasa
every evening	maiban
every week	maishuu
every month	maitsuki
every year	mainen

Time of day

morning	asa
a.m.	gozen
noon	hiru
p.m./afternoon	gogo
evening	yuugata
night	yoru

Relative time

now	ima
soon	sugu
later	atode
a little later	sukoshi atode
fast/early	hayai
quickly/in a hurry	hayaku
slow/late	osoi
slowly/late	osoku
take your time/leisurely	yukkuri
always	itsumo
sometimes	tokidoki
often	yoku
how long? (does it take?)	dono kurai

Indexed vocabulary list

Most of the individual and compound words that appear in the book are listed below. Numbers from 1 to 21 refer to chapters -see the relevant word lists. From 23 onwards, they refer to phrase numbers.

Words with index numbers highlighted in **bold** type appear repeatedly throughout the book.

Some words, for example 'area code', are grouped under a general heading, in this case 'telephone', rather than being given an individual entry. Use this method to search for words that cannot be found in the general alphabetical listing.

Indexed vocabulary list